EMOTIONALLY FREE

Emotionally Free

RITA BENNETT

KINGSWAY PUBLICATIONS
EASTBOURNE

First published in the USA by Fleming H. Revell Co.,
Old Tappan, New Jersey
First British edition 1982
Reprinted 1983 (twice)
Reprinted 1984
Reprinted 1985

ISBN 0 86065 194 0

Cover photo: Tony Stone Photolibrary—London

Printed in Great Britain for
KINGSWAY PUBLICATIONS LTD
Lottbridge Drove, Eastbourne, E. Sussex BN23 6NT by
Richard Clay (The Chaucer Press) Ltd, Bungay, Suffolk

TO the memory of my mother

LORETTA JESSE REED

who somehow planted in me the idea
that I could do
anything I decided to

Contents

Preface

This is a book about people, by people, and for people. It tells about real people with real problems, and how they found the answers.

It's a book about people being healed in their souls. I'm excited about it because of the new freedom coming in people's lives psychologically and spiritually, and also because we are seeing physical healing, sometimes from long-standing illnesses.

You may be familiar with the books my husband, Dennis, and I have authored. The teachings presented in those books are foundational to this one. In this book I'm sharing with you some new insights and answers I've found, trusting they will help you as they've helped me and others. It includes a number of prayers to assist you as you go along. There are suggestions given here which, if applied, can be life changing.

For several years we have been presenting seminars in various parts of the country and the world on the topic of the "Healing of the Whole Person." This book is comprised of the teaching given at the seminars, but in greater detail. Reading it is like sharing in an extended seminar with us, only at your own pace.

Though this book was actually written in approximately six months, I've been living it and teaching it consistently for four years. I offer it to you as a gift of love. Receive what you find in it for you, and like chaff in the wind, with a breath of kindness, blow the rest away.

Soul healing is one of those simple, logical truths that belongs to all Christians. Numerous books have been written on it, many of which have been helpful to me. Though I'm not writing on a new subject, it's new in that I'm telling it from my own viewpoint and experience, with fresh insights the Lord has been giving me. I'm glad this time I'm the one who's privileged to share it.

RITA BENNETT

Acknowledgments

First of all, bundles of thanks and appreciation go to my dear husband, Dennis, who went beyond the call of duty to give me time for this writing project. "Beyond the call" included taking over kitchen duty for a month! He and Brother Lawrence have something in common! He's anticipating my taking over the cooking now that the project is completed! (He really did very well.) Dennis's collaboration and editorial assistance was invaluable.

Very special thanks to my good friends Shade O'Driscoll and Janet Biggart, who lived much of this book with me, giving freely of themselves to others.

Hearty thanks to Sue Williams, my secretary, who's always willing to do those little extra things that mean a lot.

Loving appreciation to Hope Howard, who helped in various ways, from trips to the library to gardening.

Sincere thanks to all the soul-healing counselors in the Seattle area and throughout the USA, and especially to the group at Saint Luke's, who give willingly of themselves to pray for others, and for assisting us at our seminars.

Most of all—glory, honor, and praise to our Lord Jesus Christ, from whom all healings come.

1

The Beginning

One frosty Sunday morning in December of 1977, my husband, Dennis, intercepted me after church, looking worried. "Honey," he said, "I need your help. There's a woman—a real fine person—who's had four nervous breakdowns and it looks like she's getting ready for another. Meg[1] needs help and she needs it fast! I've counseled a lot with her in the past, but you know with my schedule I can't tackle any more right now. Would you be willing to work with her?"

I took his hand as we walked along. "I'm sure willing to do what I can," I said, "but it sounds to me as though she needs a psychiatrist." We went down the steps into the basement of the church where the after-service coffee hour was just winding up. Dennis held the door open for me. "She's been to several psychiatrists, and I'm sure they've done her some good, but I think she needs spiritual help for her problems."

Dennis knew I'd counseled many people during the seventeen years since my renewal in the Spirit, but this seemed a bit heavy. "Tell you what," I said, dropping a tea bag into my cup, and filling it with hot water from the urn on the counter, "I'll take it on, if I can find someone to work with me."

Dennis looked relieved. "Good," he replied, "I'll let her know as soon as you're ready."

Bob Peel, the sexton, appeared from the kitchen where the

volunteer crew was cleaning up and putting away, "Don't you folks have a home?" he quipped, with a grin.

"Right, Bob," said Dennis, "lunchtime was long ago and nearly everyone's gone but us. Come to think of it, I'm hungry!" He took my arm. "Let's go, honey. It's been a busy morning. See you around, Bob." We walked up the steps, climbed into our cozy red VW Rabbit, and headed for home.

Next morning I telephoned Shade O'Driscoll. Her husband, Dick, had come to Seattle and Saint Luke's as associate priest in 1967, the year after Dennis and I were married. Shade and I had known one another slightly years before, and now we had become close friends.

"Shadie," I said, "would you be interested in helping me?" I outlined Dennis's request.

"I am interested," said Shade after a few moments consideration. "Yes, I'd like to help you work with Meg."

"You know, Shade," I said, "I've been reading that book you gave me for my birthday, the one on 'inner healing.' I think it might just be what's needed."

"I think so, too," Shade replied. "You know Dick and I have been praying about some of his past hurts this way, and we're seeing exciting results." We finished our conversation, and I called Meg to arrange for the three of us to get together.

Our First Meeting With Meg

We decided to meet Meg in a room at church. Shade and I got there a little early so we could pray for the guidance of the Holy Spirit. We knew we'd have to rely on Him all the way, because this kind of praying was new to both of us, especially me.

At the appointed time, Meg knocked timidly on the half-opened door. She was a sweet-faced person in her early forties, the wife of a professional man in the community. Her head was covered with a plaid scarf, her face was pale, and she looked weighed down and tired from lack of sleep. We greeted her and invited her to take a seat between us. She smiled and sat down, slipping off her scarf and brown jacket.

"Meg, we're not going to counsel you in the usual way," Shade began in her gentle southern accent. "In fact it will be more prayer than counseling. We're not here to give you a lot of good advice. We're going to ask our risen Lord Jesus to heal you. We want to help you see Him more clearly in your life. We'll be able to help only as we let the Holy Spirit guide. He's the One who can get to the root of your problems.

"When we pray for Jesus to heal physical sickness, we aren't practicing medicine. So when we pray for the healing of your emotions, we're not trying to practice psychology or psychiatry. We're going to trust the Holy Spirit to bring to your mind any hurtful memories so Jesus can heal them. Does that sound all right?"

"Why, yes," Meg answered, hope beginning to dawn in her pretty blue eyes, "in fact it sounds wonderful!"

I leaned forward in my chair. "Meg, I'd like to ask you, who's the first person you felt really loved you? I don't want you to say who you *think* loved you because of the good things they did for you, or because they were supposed to love you. Who did you really *feel* loved you?"

I leaned back, waiting for her answer. Several years before, at a meeting in Atlanta, I'd heard the well-known writer and counselor Keith Miller ask the group, "Who was the first person, *other than your parents,* you felt really loved you? How did they express their love?" He got some interesting responses: "They held my hand," "They looked into my eyes," "They listened to me," "They said they would stand by me." Love is expressed more clearly by action than words. Perhaps our caring, listening, and praying would also convey healing love to Meg.

"My parents took good care of me, Rita, and I know they loved me, but I don't *feel* they did." Meg's eyes misted as she continued, "My parents were very busy people and didn't seem to have time for me." She paused. "The first person I felt really loved me, I guess, was a Sunday-school teacher. Her name was Dora. I was a little terror in class, and she didn't have any reason to be fond of me, but from the first moment I walked into her room I just felt sort of washed in love and accepted. And she kept on loving me, no matter how I acted."

"You didn't have a happy childhood, then?" I asked.

"No, I can't say that I did."

"Could you share with us one of the first scenes you recall which hurt you?"

"I was only three years old," Meg said, after a few moment's thought, "when one evening I came into the living room, and was scared when I heard my parents arguing loudly. I rushed over to my dad, protectively grabbed his big leg, and said, 'Don't hurt my daddy!'

"My parents stopped arguing, and began laughing. I knew they were laughing at me, and I didn't know why. I felt what I know now as ridicule. I realize how funny it must have seemed, but to me it was not funny at all. Neither of my parents picked me up or touched me, but just continued their argument, hardly missing a beat. I wandered out of the room feeling totally rejected."

"Might this be a good place to begin praying?" I asked, looking at Shade. She nodded and picked up the theme:

"Meg, let's pray about this memory. Don't worry. Things aren't going to hurt as they did the first time around, because this time we're going to let Jesus deal with it.

"Will you try to see Jesus in that scene with your folks? Just let the Holy Spirit guide you. You may see Jesus clearly or just as a faint outline. He may be dressed as you would picture

Him in the Bible, or He may be in modern clothes, or you may just feel His warmth and peace."

We moved our chairs closer and joined hands. "Jesus," Shade said, "let Meg see that You are there with her, loving her, that night when her parents were fighting."

"Can you see the scene?" Shade asked, after a few minutes. Meg closed her eyes. "Oh, yes, I can, vividly."

"Can you see Jesus, or if you can't see Him, can you sense His presence?"

"I can see Jesus and sense His presence."

"Wonderful! Where is He?"

"He's standing to the right of me. Now He's stooping down to pick me up in His arms, and saying, 'I won't leave you. I will never forsake you.' "

"How does that make the little Meg feel?"

"Oh, so much better. I feel so protected," she said, tears spilling over. I rummaged some tissues from my purse and handed them to her. We learned right from the first, a box of tissues is an important accessory!

We waited to let her bask in the comfort of Jesus' love. When the tears had subsided, Shade asked, "Now that Jesus has healed you, do you think you can tell your parents you forgive them?"

"I was thinking I should do that. Yes."

"As a responsible adult Christian, you've probably already tried to forgive your parents and all others who've wronged you?"

"That's true."

"Now we want you to forgive them as a three-year-old, from your inner self. Forgiveness is important for the release of that little child within. As you see yourself in the scene with your parents and Jesus, speak from that reference point in the room there with them. What did you call them at that age?"

"Mom and Daddy."

"Okay. Follow me in this prayer: 'Mom and Daddy, through Jesus I forgive you for arguing in front of me, for laughing at me, and not showing me the affection I needed. You did the best you knew how. I forgive you and set you free. I will no longer hold this against you. Jesus has healed me.'"

Then Meg added spontaneously, "And Mom, I love you!" She began to weep, "Oh, I've never been able to say those words before!"

A Book of Remembrance

I hugged Meg. "Write down what Jesus did for you today," I said. "Keep a sort of journal. You can use fictitious names or initials so it will be confidential. It'll be a help to look back on in the future. The prophet Malachi says God has a book of remembrance of good things we have done (3:16); why shouldn't we have a book of remembrance of the good things He's done? And while you're at it, write down all the Scriptures you can find about God holding His children in His arms and about His love for you."

"This is a wonderful beginning," said Shade, putting her arm around Meg. "There will probably be other things God will bring to mind for us to deal with. It's going to be an adventure!"

We set up a session for the next week, said our good-byes, and went our different ways.

Learning More With Meg

Even Dennis, who is a one-man Chamber of Commerce, would have found it hard to be enthusiastic about the weather that winter day when we counseled Meg for the second time! I looked out of the window at the gray sky and thought of the sunny days of my youth in Tampa, Florida. Tampa's sister city, Saint Petersburg, gave away free newspapers on the rare days when the sun didn't shine! "Here I am in Seattle," I thought. "The rain's coming down so persistently, yet I feel warm and happy. I'd rather be here doing what I'm doing than anywhere else in the world."

A Second Prayer

I was recalled from my ponderings by the entrance of Shade and Meg. As we sat down Shade asked, "How did things go this week, Meg?"

"Real good!" she said, smiling a little shyly, as she took off her green and white plaid scarf. "I really feel I got healed from my folks laughing at me that time. And you know this week I remembered another incident when I felt ridiculed. But it's much later. In fact I was eighteen, a senior in high school. Is it okay to pray about that now or should we wait until later?"

"I guess the Holy Spirit doesn't have to work in chronological order," Shade responded. "Let's take it as He brings it up."

"I was in chemistry class," Meg related. "My blue lab notebook was lying on my desk. I walked away for a few minutes, and noticed two fellows come up, one after the other, open my notebook, and write in it. I pretended not to notice, but of course I was very curious, and as soon as I could get back to my desk I opened the book, trying to look casual. I saw that the first boy had written, SHE'S NICE. The second one had written, SHE'S NUTS!

"All I could think of was that second boy's words, SHE'S NUTS! I was devastated! What I had always suspected about myself was confirmed in writing.

"I controlled myself until I got home; then I burst into tears, and cried so hard it seemed to come all the way from my toes.

There was no one at home, so I just sobbed it out by myself for three solid hours. I never felt free to tell my parents about this experience."

After Meg finished her story, we sat quietly for a few moments. Then I asked, "Would you let Jesus be Lord of that event?"

"Yes, I would," she replied.

"Let's pray, then. 'Jesus, we know you were in that chemistry lab with Meg. Help her to be aware of your healing presence.' " I reached over and took Meg's hand. "When you can, describe what you see happening."

Meg bowed her head for a few moments, but as she was contemplating, Shade began to smile, and then to laugh softly. God was giving her knowledge, one of the gifts of the Spirit. "I see *Jesus* walking up to Meg's book to write something in it," she said happily. "The students are standing around to see what it will be. Jesus opens the book and writes just two words: SHE'S MINE."

Meg began to weep, deeply moved that Jesus would do such a loving thing. Shade continued, "Now I see you looking up into His face and you're saying something to Him. Do you know what it is?"

Meg's tears subsided, and she smiled brightly as she responded without hesitation, "I'm Yours!"

Then the tears flowed again as she added, "I haven't said those words to Jesus in quite that way before, although I've known Him for many years."

My own heart glowed as I saw again what Jesus was ready to do, and how simply He did it.

"Now let's go back to the chemistry lab and see what Jesus will say to those boys," I said. I asked Meg what she felt Jesus was saying to the boy who was nice to her.

She smiled again and responded, " 'I think you have very good judgment!' Oh," she said, "now He's looking at the other fellow—the one who wrote SHE'S NUTS! He's putting His arm around him and saying, 'I know how difficult things have been for you. You've been hurt, so you strike out at others. You need to know I love you, too.' "

"Okay," said Shade. "Now let's forgive that fellow. See yourself at eighteen, and say to him, through Jesus, 'I forgive you, Joe,[2] and set you free. I will no longer hold this against you. I set myself free—free to love everyone, including you.' "

Meg repeated the prayer, her face shining.

"Do you know where Joe is?" I asked.

Meg shook her head. "I have no idea. Never saw him after we graduated."

"Well, why don't you pray that he will come to know Jesus, if he doesn't already," I said, and Meg added that petition.

"But I know the other fellow has died, the one who wrote the good words," said Meg, sadly. "What can I do about him?"

"Well, you can't speak directly to him, but let's assume that he's with Jesus, and ask Jesus to tell him what it is you want to say to him."

Meg's eyes widened a bit. "I would never have thought of that," she said, "but it makes sense. Okay. Lord, if that boy—I don't even remember his name—who was nice to me, is with You, please give him my love, and thank him for me for what he did. Thank You, Jesus!" Meg dropped her hands in her lap. "Whew! I sure do feel good about *that!* You know," she went on, "I guess I was so crushed by the unkind words Joe wrote about me, I'd never been free until now to appreciate the other boy's good words."

We've found this consistently true in soul-healing prayer: as old wounds are healed, good memories begin to be restored. We finished our time that day by going back to the scene of the grief-stricken Meg at her house and letting Jesus heal that also.

More healing was going to be needed, as Meg had suffered

much both as a child and as an adult, but these two incidents had been healed. She was on her way. As we continued to pray together, and let Jesus heal more of her past hurts, Meg's appearance began to change in a way that was obvious to everyone. She didn't have the fifth nervous breakdown that had been predicted. She put away her head scarf, got a new hairdo, and began teaching Sunday school at her church! Everyone could see the difference in her. Eventually she herself began to help pray with others.

When I wrote Meg asking permission to use her story in this book, she commented, "Do you know the healings Jesus did are so good that although I remember the incidents it's become hard for me to remember the details. I haven't forgotten the things that happened, but they've been reduced to proper size. I can even see the humor in them!"

Workers Needed for the Harvest

"Rita," Shade said after we'd bid a happy farewell to Meg, "you know the needs are so great, we could have a line of people a block long waiting for help. Some are already asking to be put on the waiting list. We need to do something. Let's pray and ask God to send others, men and women, to work with us."

"Good idea," I replied. "We're just two people and busy ones at that."

There was a knock on the door and Dennis poked his head in to see if I was ready to go home. The three of us joined hands. "Dear God," we prayed, "You know the needs in Your Body in this world. The things that hinder Your Kingdom coming to earth in and through us are so interwoven and hidden, only You can show us what they are. and release us from them. Father, You told us to pray for workers in the harvest, and we're doing that now. The three of us agree, asking You to call and equip people to bring wholeness to Your Body and to the world, in Jesus' name."

We hugged one another (I call it a holy huddle), and went home, assured that God had heard us. All we had to do was take the next step He showed. We didn't have to see the whole picture. We didn't know then, but it was the beginning of something wonderful for us, our church, and the world we would touch.

2

Jim Moves Ahead

Dennis had just finished greeting the people from the ten o'clock service. There was a promise of spring in the air. He stood for a moment on the church steps, took a deep breath of the freshness, then turned and walked back inside the building. Someone was still kneeling at the altar. It was Jim,[2a] a longtime church member and friend.

"Hi," Dennis said, walking down the aisle toward him. "Can I help?" He knelt down beside him.

Jim, a good-looking man in his late thirties, shrugged his shoulders. "You asked Lisa[2b] and me to come to the altar after the service to pray for people, but when I got here I realized I'm the one who needs prayer. I've been discouraged and depressed for some months now, without any cause I know of. I'm happily married—you know that. Lisa's a wonderful wife. We have three beautiful kids. I'm satisfied with my work and I love this church."

Jim paused a moment, then continued: "I thought maybe I was being hassled by some kind of demonic influence, you know, and I've rebuked that, but still no change. I've tried repeating victory Scriptures and affirmations of faith. That's been a lifesaver for me before, but now it doesn't seem to work. I pray in the Spirit and try to 'praise God anyway,' but I only get a temporary lift.

"After I accepted Jesus and the power of the Holy Spirit, life

28

was exciting; now it's settled down to a dull routine. Some of the people I listen to on my tape recorder say that's the way it is; you're *supposed* to cool down; you can't stay in the Spirit—but I can't accept that. I don't expect to be tooling around on cloud nine all the time, but I'd like to be happy in my heart. I can't seem to get hold of God the way I once did.

"And it isn't just the dullness," Jim went on. "Some of my old fears and insecurities seem to be coming back. Frustration, anger, rejection—I thought I'd left it all behind, but now I don't know."

How Jim Came to Saint Luke's

Jim? Having problems? Dennis's mind flashed back fifteen years to when Jim had first come to the church, so upset and tense he could barely function. He'd been going from one doctor to another, and trying one medication after another. As Jim put it:

"I went from doctor to doctor in hopes of solving my problem, but no one understood. I had chest pains and went to my family doctor. He said it was tension and referred me to a psychiatrist, who in turn sent me to a neurologist. He stuck electrodes on my head, and decided I probably had some rare disease—only I didn't have the rest of the symptoms! Then I went back to the psychiatrist, who said he could find nothing psychologically wrong with me—he just gave me drugs. I had bad reactions to every one of them, which caused me further troubles."

Jim's wife had attended a local community college. One of the professors had had a life-changing experience himself. He told Jim about it, and urged him to come to the church on a Friday night. Jim did, received Christ and the release of the Holy Spirit, and literally became a new person. The metamorphosis had been so complete that Jim, who had been so insecure he was afraid to open his mouth in public, now became so confident he kidded the prof, saying he could even handle being president of Boeing Aviation, where he was then working!

Jim had seemed happy and relaxed through the years that followed. He'd moved ahead in his work, and now was a sales representative with a large company. It was hard to believe he still had problems, but Dennis concealed his surprise and said nothing, so Jim went on.

"I've been hearing about this inner healing and the idea bothers me. People are saying negative things about it, like 'If you're a new creature in Christ why should you still need to have inner healing?' On the other hand, I have a funny feeling God may be telling me it's what I need, but I'm saying 'no way!' The idea threatens my security. I'm afraid to look at my fears."

Dennis put his hand on Jim's shoulder. "I don't know about you, Jim, but I'm certainly being helped by it. Only I like to call it *soul healing.*"

It was now Jim's turn to be surprised. "You?" he said.

Dennis laughed. "Oh, yeah, I know. Pastors aren't supposed to have problems, and often manage to give the impression they don't, but believe me, they do, and I'm no different. Sure, we all need help from time to time."

Jim went home to think it over. *So Dennis believes in this soul-healing stuff? He's always been so balanced and scriptural. Maybe there's something to it. If God's in this, I'm sure not going to let people's mistakes or prejudices keep me from it.*

It wasn't long before Dennis got a call from Jim saying he, too, would like to have some help.

"Rita and Shade have been getting good results," Dennis

said. "Would you mind having a couple of gals pray with you?"

"Nope," Jim said. "That's no problem."

"In general, I like to have men, or a man and woman, pray with men," said Dennis, "but we don't as yet have any doing this kind of work." So Dennis referred Jim to Shade and me, and near the end of February 1978, we had our first meeting.

Where should we begin? Prayer for soul healing is not "poor man's psychiatry." We don't "dig around," but we pray and trust the Holy Spirit to guide us to the problems, so Jesus can heal them. With Meg, I asked her a question: "Who was the first person you felt really loved you?" With Jim we were led to a slightly different approach.

"You already received a lot of soul healing when you came to the Lord," I said. "Why don't you tell us something about yourself before that time."

Jim began to talk about his background:

I was brought up in a logging community with a lot of tough-minded people. Why, [laughing] one of my relatives cut his leg with a chain saw—really laid it open—but he didn't go to the doctor. No, he sewed it up himself, and went on working! I felt I had to be tough like them. I didn't do well in grade school. It was no wonder after high school I got in with a rough group of kids whose lives revolved around three things: hot-rod racing, drinking, and girls. This crowd made me feel accepted. They didn't demand anything of me, nor I of them. I began to settle down a bit after I graduated and had to get out and make a living. Then, fortunately, Lisa came into my life. And then Jesus!

But I don't understand. When my life changed I thought all my fears were taken care of, yet I have to admit I'm still afraid of a lot of things. Maybe somebody's going to ask me to go on a missionary journey to another country, and I'd be scared to do that. I have a fear that something would happen that I couldn't handle. Yet I'm supposed to be strong like my childhood male image.

"The obvious things were taken care of when you received Jesus and were released in the Holy Spirit," Shade put in, "those Jesus could reach at the time. But if you're like the rest of us, you have stuff tucked away which hasn't yet been opened to Jesus, sometimes because we don't even know about it; sometimes because we are subconsciously guarding it and keeping it hidden. Jesus knows it's there, of course, but He needs our consent before He can deal with it."

In soul-healing prayer we may spend time just talking, getting to know the person and his or her background, finding clues where the Holy Spirit wants us to begin. With Jim, we found in childhood he suffered from dyslexia. Dyslexia is a learning disability: "the inability to process language symbols."[3] This was the major reason he hadn't done well in grade school.

Some well-known people are believed to have suffered from dyslexia—Albert Einstein, for example. It's amazing to realize that Einstein, perhaps the greatest mathematical physicist who ever lived, was in his youth a poor reader, and he flunked algebra!

Nowadays, early diagnosis and assistance from knowledgeable and caring doctors, educators, and psychologists would have minimized the harm. But the syndrome was not understood when Jim was a child. It was a perfect situation for heartaches to occur, especially in school.

School Days

"I hated school from first grade until the last day of high school," Jim said. "Second grade was the worst. I learned never to open my mouth to ask questions. One day my teacher ridiculed me in front of the class. We were taking a test, and under tension I would often blank out. Auditory dyslexia, which was part of my problem, makes it difficult to process information, so I didn't understand the instructions. I wasn't able to do the test, so I just sat there in frustration and cried. The teacher announced to the class, 'All Jim knows how to do is *cry* through his test.' "

"How did that make you feel?" Shade asked.

"Well, like a dummy—and no good. I just hated myself."

"Okay, this is a good place to begin. Can you visualize that classroom, Jim?"

Jim closed his eyes. "Yes," he said. "I see myself there feeling humiliated and crying. The room seems dark."

"Jesus was there, wasn't He?" Shade went on.

"Oh, yes, I realize He was with me then, only I didn't know it."

"Can you visualize Him?"

Jim nodded. "Uh-huh. He's walking into the dark room; there's light all around Him. Now He's coming over to my desk." Jim's voice took on a little excitement. "He's kneeling down beside me."

"What's He saying to you?"

"He says His love for me will help me learn, and help me accept myself. He says He'll make me able to forgive my teacher, too."

"All right," said Shade. "Then let's do just that. As you see yourself back in the classroom, I want you, as a second-grader, through Jesus, to speak to your teacher. Say 'Teacher, I forgive you for making fun of me in front of the class, and I won't hold it against you anymore. I set you free, and I set myself free, too. In Jesus' name.' "

Jim followed Shade in the prayer, then grinned suddenly. "Hey!" he said. "When I forgave my teacher, the whole room suddenly lit up. It isn't dark at all anymore. It's full of light!

"Now Jesus is going to the blackboard with me. With Him I'm not afraid to work in front of the class. Boy, He sure is a good teacher!"

Unlocked

Other needs began to emerge as we talked and prayed together. Once again we realized, as with Meg, how seemingly trivial and childish incidents could affect a person's whole life. Jim remembered, when he was a first-grader, a couple of sixth-grade boys threatened him when he was alone in the rest room.

"What did they say they were going to do to you?" I asked.

Jim hesitated. "They said . . . they were going to lock me in."

"Can you see Jesus in that scene?" I asked.

"Oh, yes, I see Him there, and now the boys are leaving."

"All right, Jim," I said. "Let's see what Jesus will do about it. Just watch Him!"

Jim started to chuckle. "Oh," he said, "He's got a big key. He says there isn't anything He can't unlock! He says He can walk through any closed door, if He wants to. He's coming over to me, and is unlocking a big padlock that goes around my chest. Wow, Jesus turned the key and the lock just fell off! You know what? He shows me the words those boys scared me with had me locked into many fears, but now the lock is gone. I sure feel a weight has dropped off me!"

"Good, Jim," I went on, "now let's get rid of those words. Follow me in this prayer:

"In the name of Jesus I bind the words spoken to me, 'We're

going to lock you in.' I command these words to be powerless in my life and to influence me no more consciously or subconsciously. I claim my freedom through Jesus. *Amen.*"

"And what about the boys?" I asked, when we had finished the prayer.

Jim looked surprised. "Oh didn't I tell you? When Jesus and I walked out of the rest room the boys were standing there. With Him I wasn't afraid, so I hugged them and they hugged me back!"

"That's great," Shade offered, "but it might be a good idea to speak forgiveness to those fellows just the same."

"Oh, gosh," he said, "I wouldn't have the least idea where they are. I don't even know *who* they are."

"That doesn't matter; Jesus knows. See yourself as the first-grader, and tell them you forgive them."

Jim hesitated a moment, then he said, "Okay, you kids who threatened to lock me in that rest room, I forgive you! I won't hold this against you anymore. Through Jesus I say this." When he was through, he looked up with a smile of relief: "Hey, I feel even better! Praise the Lord!

"You know there's something else I'm seeing," he went on. "I've always been afraid to change my pattern of doing things. Once I start doing something one way, I'm really scared to alter it. This is even true in my spiritual life. I'm afraid to change the way I pray, or the things I do for the church. I'm always afraid I'll get out of God's will, and Satan will attack me.

"People with dyslexia tend to stick to a pattern for dear life, and it's hard to change. When I came to Jesus I locked into a new pattern and found security there. Now I see when Jesus unlocked that padlock He set me free to be flexible. I think things are going to be different."

"Turn the Hearts of the Children . . ."

Lorin Cunningham, founder and director of "Youth With A Mission," speaking for a rally in Seattle, put it succinctly: "The need to forgive usually begins with our parents because they are closest to us and we were most dependent on them." We discovered the truth of this again while praying with Jim. I'm not encouraging blame of parents for your problems, but if parents aren't psychologically aware and/or Spirit-filled and Spirit-led Christians, children get hurt. When you acknowledge the hurts and let Jesus heal them, love for parents can be restored, or even created for the first time, which will "turn the hearts of the fathers to the children, and the hearts of the children to their fathers . . ." (Malachi 4:6). Soul-healing prayer can help that happen.

The next time we prayed, the Holy Spirit took us to a memory when Jim was only three years old. About this time, his father accepted a job with a federal construction project which required him to travel a good deal. At first he was away for a full three weeks, and after that he could only come home weekends. Jim's parents didn't know how to explain to their three-year-old what was going on. Perhaps they thought he was too young to understand. "I used to meet my dad at the door every night when he came home from work," said Jim. "I'd bring him his slippers. I can still remember that first night when I went to the door, slippers in hand, and opened it to emptiness, darkness, and no Daddy." This had happened several evenings in succession, and had been devastating to the sensitive child. "I thought, *If Dad isn't coming home, maybe my mother will be the next to leave,*" said Jim.

We prayed through these times to help the little Jim within the big Jim. He revisualized the initial scene. "There's still a dark, empty hole as I open the door," he said, "but I know

Jesus is there. Oh, now it's growing lighter. Jesus is standing there, smiling at me! He's picked me up and He's telling me it's okay—my daddy will be coming home soon. He's helping me understand."

We encouraged Jim, as he saw himself at the age of three, to speak forgiveness to his parents. "Through Jesus, Mom and Dad, I forgive you for not knowing how to prepare me for Dad's change of jobs. You did the best you knew how. I set you both free, and I set myself free. I won't hold this against you any longer. Jesus has healed me."

As time went on, Jim related more to us about his early years. "Because my dad was away so much, I felt I was stepping into my father's role while I was still only a child. When my father came home weekends, he'd take me fishing or hunting. My mother and sister stayed at home. Though we were alone together on those occasions, my father never shared his inner feelings; therefore I didn't either. We played together on the weekends, but I rarely saw him in a father's role. His work schedule was like this from when I was three until I was seventeen. Dad tried his best to give me a good time, but not seeing him at home in a father's role didn't provide an adequate pattern for being a father myself, later on."

Jim the child had to carry an adult-size burden. He felt emotionally responsible for his mother and sister, and did all the worrying his father would have done, had he been there. Because Jim's mother was lonely, she shared with him problems which were beyond his ability to deal with.

Jim was a satisfactory person to pray with. During the week following each prayer session, he went on to let God heal other hurts. We encourage people to know they can pray soul-healing prayers for themselves. Jim always had a good report to share before we began further prayer.

Another Prayer Partner

Shade and I were new to this type of prayer, so it took longer than if we had been more experienced, though we had both done other kinds of counseling for many years. Midway through our twelve meetings with Jim, Shade and her family went on a trip to Israel, and then to Switzerland. She would be away two months. I obviously needed another partner. Shade had been telling a mutual friend, Janet Biggart, what she was learning about inner healing. Janet had had experience in other methods of prayer and counseling. She was interested in what we were doing and seemed a logical choice to take Shade's place. I felt a little insecure at first without Shade to take the lead, and realized it was time for me to try my wings. God was able to work through Janet and me as a team, even as He had with Shade.

Here was an advantage of working in twos. When Shade had to leave, I could take a new partner, fill her in on what had been going on, and even let her read my notes (which I faithfully kept). No time was lost backtracking.

Ministry to Men Is Launched

Our prayers with Jim concluded one day when he walked in and announced, "Well, I can't think of anything else to pray about!" We spent our time that day rejoicing and thanking God. One month later we met to be sure nothing had surfaced that needed further help.

Not long after we started praying with Jim, he had begun praying with someone else, applying what he was learning. He found a special empathy with those having dyslexia and other learning disabilities. He prayed with a friend and fellow churchman, for his healing, and afterward they teamed up.

The Lord was answering our prayer for "workers in His harvest," and opening the way for a men's ministry.

We found that soul-healing prayer is as helpful to a man as to a woman. A man is often schooled to put on a brave front, while inside he hurts deeply. Since he's not "supposed" to have hurts, he tends to bury them, but they don't go away; instead they may cause trouble psychologically and physically. Perhaps this is one reason men often don't live as long as women. Men tend to keep their problems to themselves, but women talk them out. Our men began to "share their burdens" with one another, as Saint Paul instructs (Galatians 6:2). They even wept together.

The good news began to spread. Other people besides Meg and Jim saw that God had help for them. Some had struggled for years, to no avail. They began to take heart: *Perhaps there's still hope for me!*

3

Psyche and Spirit

Perhaps you, at this point, are asking the same question Jim did: "If I'm a new creature in Christ, why should my inner self still need some kind of healing?" Meg and Jim had both been committed Christians for years; why would they need further healing?

When you come right down to it, though, there aren't very many of us who would claim we are perfectly whole. It's clear we do still think, and do, and say, things we ought not, and it's clear, too, we still have upset and confused feelings that trouble us from time to time. It would seem there often *is* something inside that needs healing.

The answer to this puzzle is that you are not just a two-part being, with an inner self, or soul, and an outer self, or body. The Bible mentions three parts: spirit, soul, and body. The second chapter of Genesis says, "The Lord God formed man of the dust of the ground [*body*], and breathed into his nostrils the breath of life [*spirit*]; and man became a living *soul*" (Genesis 2:7). The writer of the Book of Hebrews says that the Word of God can divide or distinguish the *soul* from the *spirit* (4:12). Paul concludes a letter to his friends in Thessalonica, ". . . may your *spirit* and *soul* and *body* be kept strong and blameless until that day when our Lord Jesus Christ comes back again" (1 Thessalonians 5:23 TLB, italics mine).

Most of the time the Old Testament emphasizes the Hebrew

view that a human being is one total person. This well-known concept has been accepted by Christians for a long time and is foundational to what I'm saying. But a house can have a number of rooms, and still be one house. Unless we grasp the New Testament picture which shows we are three-part beings, we will certainly be limiting further understanding and growth.

To give you a brief synopsis, the spirit is that part of you made in what the Scripture calls the "image" of God.[4] No, God doesn't put a little bit of Himself into each human being, but He does give each of us a spiritual nature that is made *like* Him, and therefore can respond to Him and have fellowship with Him. I believe when the first human beings turned away from God, in what we call the Fall of man, their spirits lost the ability to respond to God.

When I received Jesus, the Holy Spirit came in and brought my spirit alive to God. His image or likeness was restored in my spirit, and greatest of all miracles, He came to take up permanent residence in me. I was born again of the Spirit, "from above," as the Greek says. I became a "new creation": God's Spirit joined to my spirit. So this inmost part of me *has been* saved, restored, put back in order.

But my "soul" part is another matter. The Greek for "soul" is *psyche*. My soul is my *psych*ological nature: emotions, intellect, and will—my feelings, my thoughts, and my desires and drives. This part of me is in the process of *being* made whole, day by day. It still sometimes struggles against the Spirit of God. This is the part of which Paul said, "The good that I would I do not: but the evil which I would not, that I do" (Romans 7:19). He tells the Philippians to "work out your own salvation with fear and trembling," but he goes on to say that "it is God who is working in you both to will and to do of his good pleasure" (*see* Philippians 2:12, 13). The Lord *is* there, even though I may at times resist Him.

The word translated "save" in the New Testament, which is the Greek verb *sōzō*, has a much broader meaning in Greek than we give it in English. It does mean "brought to safety," or "rescued," but it also means "nurtured," "healed," "taken care of." If you have received Jesus, you *are* a member of the Kingdom. You are *in!* Your *spirit* has been saved, rescued. Your *soul* has been saved for eternity also, but it needs to go on being saved every day, as it learns to listen to the Spirit of God, growing stronger, defeating Satan's attacks. You'll be rescued again and again as you learn more and more to trust the Rescuer.

So it is the *soul,* or psychological nature, that needs healing from the hurts of the past. Many of these hurts are not of our doing at all. Others are from our own wrong decisions to go our own way and not God's. This book is specifically talking about the healing of the *soul,* which helps bring wholeness to the total person.

The Body

Then there is my body. This is the physical organism through which I relate to the world around me. Through it, I express myself, and through it, I receive *im*pressions from the outside world. My body is innocent. I can no more blame my body for what I do wrong than I can blame my automobile if I am caught speeding! Of course, I may have an accident if my car is defective, and I can have a difficult time driving if I am putting the wrong kind of fuel in the gas tank. So if my body is defective in some way, or I fail to provide it with proper nourishment, it can give me trouble, but that is not because of any malicious intention on its part.

The body's problems are mostly straightforward: aches, pains, injuries, diseases. Some of these problems, on the other hand, can affect the soul. Low blood sugar can make a person nervous or cranky. Liver-related disease can bring depression. Too much sugar or caffeine may cause hyperactivity.

It may be by such things as choosing bad nutrition, neglecting exercise, or through abuse by narcotics or drugs that the soul is affected. But most of the traffic is in the other direction; it is mainly the soul that affects the body. Hurts in the soul can get in God's way as He seeks to keep the body healthy, or to heal it if it gets sick.

God wants to heal His people—the Bible leaves us in no doubt at all about that—but the Holy Spirit is often hampered from healing our bodies. The healing of the soul can open the way to the healing of the body, sometimes dramatically. Though this concept is not a total answer to physical healing, we have seen people's bodies instantly healed when they allowed Jesus to heal their souls.

Problems of the Soul

Many of the soul's problems lie on the surface: for example, anger and fear in the emotions; confusion in the intellect; indecision and frustration in the will. These you can recognize and, to a certain extent at least, deal with. But you know, if you have been trying to grow in the Spirit, sometimes you cannot make the headway you'd like to. You can see what is wrong, and what needs to be corrected in your life, but somehow you cannot find out how to correct it.

This is because there is in each of us a vast area called the unconscious or subconscious, which we are not able to reach directly. This subconscious is part of the soul. Some teach that the subconscious is the spirit part of us, but I don't see it this way. It would have to be holy, as God is, for Him to dwell there. God does not enter our lives through the subconscious, and then work His way into our consciousness. He touches us in our spirits, and when we open up to Him and receive Him, He comes to live there. He can then begin to deal with our souls, including the subconscious part.

The mind has been compared to an iceberg. The top (the part you can see) is like the conscious mind, which is aware of itself, and of the things around it. The iceberg below the surface is like the subconscious mind. Just as the iceberg below is seven times larger than that which appears above, so the unconscious part of the mind or soul is vastly larger than the conscious part. It is a great storehouse of information. Among other thoughts that are stored there are repressed memories that hurt too much, and have been put away unlabeled, so that we don't even know they are there. The most difficult problems of the soul are those things that have been forgotten, or repressed in the subconscious mind.

You see people who have been sincerely trying to live for God for many years. They make a certain amount of progress, and then they get stuck. They may find it difficult to pray or praise God, and sometimes stop communicating with Him altogether. They find bitterness welling up from within them, so that the healing flow of the Spirit is checked. They can't seem by any means to make further headway against their problems.

This is because of the "hidden agenda"—hurts in the depths of the soul that have been locked away, so that even the Holy Spirit cannot touch them; for God needs us to release things to Him willingly before He can deal with them. I think it was Watchman Nee who said that neither God nor the devil could do anything in our lives without first obtaining our consent, because man's will is free.

In 1951, Dr. Wilder Penfield, a neurosurgeon at McGill University in Montreal, carried out a series of experiments with the memory during brain surgery. He found that stimulating certain areas caused the patient to recall an incident vividly, as if it were being reënacted. This was not so surprising, for it had long been recognized that our brains record everything that happens to us. What was interesting, though, was that not only was the incident recalled, but also the emotions associated with it. It wasn't just the event that was reënacted in memory, but how the person *felt* about that event, and how he or she interpreted the meaning of the event. Dr. Penfield says, "The subject feels again the emotion which the situation originally produced in him, and he is aware of the same interpretations, true or false, which he himself gave to the experience in the first place. Thus, evoked recollection is not the exact photographic or phonographic reproduction of past scenes or events. It is reproduction of what the patient saw and heard, felt and understood."[5]

The event, the feelings, and the interpretation seem to be permanently joined together—and therefore recalled together. Thus scientific experiment shows that the past lives on in us whether we consciously remember it or not. It is not the memory of the event itself that hurts us as much as the memory of our feelings about and our interpretation of the event. Hurts of the past that have sunk into the subconscious may continue to cause pain without our knowing where it comes from, and may cause us to react in ways we don't mean to, or may even cause physical illness.

Everything that has happened to you, even from the time you were a tiny baby, is recorded in your memory—not only the events, but also how they made you feel. It is those feelings, much more than the memory of the events themselves, which can hinder you in the present from moving as freely in the life of the Spirit as you would like to, and can affect you physically or psychologically. As we are open to God, He can reveal such hidden agenda so that it, too, can be healed.

Rocks in Your River

Sometimes in spring or early summer, Dennis and I go up to the Skykomish River in the mountains, not far from where we live. At that time of year, the river will be nearly bankfull, a smooth flow of dark-green water. If we go back in the late summer, the river will have dropped, and instead of the smooth water gliding along, we will see rocks, the water going around them and between them and under them, trying to find its way to the sea. There will be waves and eddies and bursts of spray and foam as the river struggles with the obstacles in its path. Now, if we want to strengthen the flow of the water, we will need to dig out the rocks; *then* the water can once again flow swiftly and smoothly.

That's the way it is with the flow of God's Spirit through the soul. There are times when the Holy Spirit is moving so strongly that nothing holds Him back. You may have had this experience when you were first released in the Spirit, or when you have been at a meeting where your spirit has been strongly stimulated. At times like these, you aren't aware of the rocks in the streambed. But inevitably there come times when you aren't moving so strongly in the Holy Spirit—not because *He* is holding back, but perhaps because you are not attending to Him, but rather to the things around you in the world; therefore you are not allowing the Holy Spirit to flow freely into your soul. You get (quite literally) "spiritually dry." At such times you can become very much aware of the rocks in the streambed, and the need to get rid of them. Some of the rocks could block the source of the stream, so there's no flow at all. So we can have God in our spirits, and yet resist Him and block His work in our souls and bodies.

When the rocks of pride, greed, misunderstanding, hate, anger, unforgiveness (you name them) show up, they need to be removed. Even if the water is still flowing strongly, so you're not too aware of the rocks, wouldn't it still be good to get rid of them and let the flow be stronger yet?

Some of these blockages are from our own sins, and the remedy is repentance. Even though we are Christians, we still need to come to God for cleansing. Then He reaches down into the stream and throws out the rocks.

In soul healing, however, we're not so much focusing on the rocks that *we* have dropped in our river, acts we have knowingly and intentionally done which require us to repent, change our ways, and receive God's forgiveness. If we aren't already dealing with these to the best of our ability, we haven't really started on the Christian trail. In soul healing, we are mainly concerned with the rocks that have been dropped into our stream of life by *others*. Some have been thrown in maliciously, some knocked in accidentally because of someone walking along carelessly. There are also things that have happened to us that weren't anyone's fault, natural events and crises which, like a landslide caused by wind or water, pour debris into the stream of our souls.

No matter how these rocks may have gotten into your life, you need to be free of them. So let God reveal the hurts and you, with His help and direction, throw out whatever is impeding the flow of the Spirit. It will be to your great benefit.

If God's Holy Spirit is living in your spirit, from there the new life can flow out into your soul, so that both the conscious and unconscious parts can be healed and flow together in Him.

4

Do You Need Soul Healing?

SOLE TALK

People's souls are often like shoe soles:

Some are thick skinned,
Others are thin.

Many are worn-out,
Others hurt because they're flat.

Some are out of step,
Others are lost.

Many are cold,
Others are empty.

Some do a lot of kicking,
Others are footloose, and fancy they're free.

Many need support,
Others act like heels.

But some are in good repair:
They warm themselves in the "Son"
And carry their weight,
They toe the line,
Then run a good race.

RITA BENNETT

"What is soul-healing prayer?"

"Do I need soul healing?"

"How can I receive it?"

"What can I do to help other people get healed?"

"How did you get into the ministry of inner healing?"

These are some of the questions I'm asked, and I'll answer for you in this book.

If you ask ten different people what inner healing or soul healing is, you might get ten different answers. They could all be correct, too, as each person would be looking at the subject from his or her own experience.

To me it is God restoring your soul as you learn to practice the presence of Jesus in the past, as well as in the present, and on into the future—helping you to forgive everyone, and setting you free to live at your fullest potential.

"A tall order," you may say. Maybe you won't walk this way constantly, but there are moments when it is possible, and the moments can turn into hours, and hours into days, as you reach for a goal which God has for you. A goal must be something you reach for or you won't stretch and grow.

No, it doesn't happen overnight, but we've been watching people change, sometimes slowly, sometimes with amazing suddenness, as their souls are healed. Jesus is the same in the past, present, and future (*see* Hebrews 13:8). God has been with you always, and He's with you now, but you have to "practice" realizing His presence.

In the previous chapter, I used the illustration of blocks in the soul being like rocks in a riverbed. There we saw that soul healing is removing the rocks, so the Spirit of God can flow through our souls without obstruction.

Hope Howard, a daughter in Christ, describes the need for soul healing this way: "It's like having garbage in your kitchen," she says, "and instead of getting rid of it, you throw it into the basement!" As I thought about Hope's apt description, I realized that most of the garbage we're talking about in soul healing isn't from our own kitchen—it's been contributed by others! So I expanded her illustration a bit.

A person comes to your front door and knocks. You open it, and they hand you a bag of garbage. Not knowing what else to do, you accept it. Someone else knocks at the door, and the scene is repeated. Some of your callers just leave the garbage on the front steps without knocking! Soon your kitchen is overflowing, so you begin to put the bags in the basement. It isn't too long before your house begins to smell horrible!

There are two things you can do. You can grow accustomed to the smell and keep stuffing things into the basement (of your subconscious); or you can call for Jesus, the One who knows how to get rid of it. Just as you can produce rich soil by composting literal garbage, so Jesus, who always knows how to make something good out of something bad, can use the hurts you have suffered to bring you good (*see* Romans 12:21). The nasty stuff people have been dumping in your life can be used by Jesus to produce good, rich soil in which your life can grow.

What Soul Healing Isn't

I'll be giving further definitions of soul-healing prayer as we go along, but now let's consider a few things it *isn't:*

1. Soul healing is *not* reconfessing past sins. Corrie ten Boom teaches that our forgiven sins are cast in the sea of God's forgetfulness, to be remembered against us no more. By the sea, she says, is a little sign: NO FISHING ALLOWED. We're certainly not doing any of *that* kind of fishing! Those sacks of garbage of our own making—ones we've confessed—have already been

handed over to Jesus. It would be silly to try to give something to Jesus that doesn't exist. However, the consequences and results of our wrongdoing, any damage done to others, require correction, and healing, too. And we often need help forgiving ourselves.

2. Soul healing *isn't* digging around in the basement of your subconscious, but letting God bring things to the main floor of your life as *He* chooses. Things which have seemingly been forgotten by the conscious mind can be festering in the unconscious, sending up all kinds of problems. God brings the buried stuff to remembrance so He can heal it; then it loses its power to hurt. He can give us new feelings about the old scenes, so that when they are remembered, the pain is gone. Not only has the wound been cleansed, it's been healed as well.

3. Soul healing *isn't* giving advice, although as you pray with people, the Holy Spirit may give clearer insight into their problems. If they're looking for advice, they should be directed to qualified professionals: pastors, marriage counselors, doctors, psychologists, or psychiatrists instead of (or in addition to) soul-healing prayer.[6]

4. Soul-healing prayer *isn't* a psychological gimmick. It doesn't give easy answers which avoid the Cross. It's a supernatural encounter with the crucified and resurrected Lord Jesus. "Certainly He has borne our griefs, and carried our sorrows. . . . He was whipped and bruised for our sins, took our punishment to bring us peace, and through His wounds we are healed" (Isaiah 53:4, 5, *paraphrased*). Any such healing received is through, in, and because of Jesus.

Did Jesus Pray This Way?

"This is all well and good," you may say, "but did Jesus ever pray for people for soul healing?"

Jesus did not need to practice "soul healing" in the way we do today, because soul healing is simply bringing the presence of Jesus into the hurtful scene, and letting Him work. So whenever anyone came into the presence of Jesus when He was living on earth, if they desired it, their soul would be healed, as well as their body and spirit.

There are numerous examples of people who came to Jesus needing their souls healed. "The woman in the city who was a sinner" (*see* Luke 7:37–50), for example, or the "certain women, which had been healed of evil spirits and infirmities" (8:2), which included Mary Magdalene. In addition to healing their bodies, Jesus forgave them their sins, cast out the evil spirits, and healed their souls. The woman who had been a prostitute no longer degraded herself by selling her love; Jesus restored her self-respect. Undoubtedly she, like the others, became His devoted follower. Mary Magdalene was the first person Jesus greeted on Resurrection Morning, according to John 20:17, 18.

The woman at the well in Samaria had had numerous husbands and was living with a man to whom she was not married. Jesus simply showed her that He knew all about her. She accepted Him immediately, and whatever in her soul caused her to go from man to man and never be able to commit herself to one person, was surely healed by the presence of Jesus. She won a whole town to Him! Our souls can be healed as we become aware that "Jesus was there," knows all about us, and loves us just the same.

One of the clearest examples of Jesus' soul healing is found in John 21, but I'll tell this in more detail in chapter 6.

Faults Need Healing

Are we supposed to pray for others for healing of their souls? The King James Version of the Scripture, James 5:16, reads,

"Confess your faults one to another, and pray for one another, that ye may be healed. . . ." Dennis says, "Almost every other translation of the New Testament reads, 'Confess your sins one to another.' The usual Greek word for 'sin' in the New Testament is *hamartia.* It occurs 172 times. But the word used in James 5:16 is *paraptoma,* which occurs only 23 times. It is translated 'sin' only four times in the King James Version. Six times it is translated 'offense,' nine 'trespasses,' twice 'fall,' and twice 'fault.' Arndt and Gingrich, in their *Greek-English Lexicon of the New Testament,* give as the first meaning of *paraptoma,* 'a false step.' It can be used to indicate an error, a mistake in judgment, a blunder."[7]

"It seems to me that the translators of the King James Version saw that it couldn't be *sins* we're to confess *to one another.* We confess our sins to *God;* and sins are not *healed,* they are *forgiven.* That's why the word is translated 'fault' rather than 'sin.' We are to admit our *faults* or weaknesses to one another, so we can pray to be *healed.*"

A "fault" is a *defect*—something you cannot help. A hurt in the soul that needs healing would be a "fault," not a sin, although if it is not healed, it can lead to sin.

If you have a faulty tire on your car, and you don't get it fixed, it may cause an accident. *Soul healing is praying for one another's faults to be healed so that there will not later be sins to be forgiven.* It's getting to the problem before the problem gets to you.

A Checklist for Soul Healing

Your soul needs healing if you have been hurt or damaged by another person, experience, or event outside your control. We're not yet living in heaven; we're exposed to the imperfections of ourselves and others, so we can safely say everyone to some degree has needed, presently needs, or will need healing for the soul.

Here is a checklist to help you recognize if you would benefit from healing prayer:

1. Were you greatly embarrassed when a child or young adult?

2. Can you see a pattern of hurtful events beginning early in your life, each building upon the other?

3. Do you have difficulty recalling anything about your childhood? Is it a total blank?

4. Do you wish you were someone else? Do you dislike yourself? Do you wish you had never been born?

5. Do you dislike the opposite sex, or your own sex?

6. Do you have a learning disability such as dyslexia, which was not diagnosed in childhood? Do you, or did you, have another kind of limiting handicap?

7. Are there habits ("besetting sins") that control you?

8. Do you have unreasonable fears?

9. Do you often find your reaction to something said or done is far beyond the stimulus?

10. Do you have a recurring memory of a past hurt? Does it still trouble you to think about it?

11. Are there people you can't forgive? Do you have trouble asking someone else to forgive you?

12. Do you have overwhelming feelings of guilt?

13. Do you find it nearly impossible to admit making a mistake? Do you usually look for someone to blame for what goes wrong in your life?

14. Do you have a nearly continuous feeling of anger inside? Are you usually critical in your remarks or thoughts about others?

15. Do you go on compulsive overeating or drinking binges? compulsive undereating binges?

16. Do you have a fantasy world you escape into?

17. Are you obsessed with sexual thoughts or fantasies?

18. Do you have a physical illness that has no known cause?

19. Do you suffer from depression frequently, or over long periods of time?

20. Do you have frequent nightmares, or troubling recurring dreams?

21. Do you have physical or mental exhaustion from wrestling with inner problems? Do you have difficulty sleeping, or do you want to sleep too much? (Check for physical causes, too.)

22. Are you extremely restless, "on the go" constantly? Unable to sit and relax from time to time? (There's a difference between a healthy "drive" and being driven.)

23. Are you a workaholic? Do you feel guilty if you aren't doing something "productive"? Are you always striving for the approval of others?

24. Were you an adult before you ever felt loved by another person?

25. Do you often compare yourself with others and end up feeling inadequate and discouraged?

26. Do you have a constant need for physical affection, or do you not like to be touched at all?

27. Do you have a deep sense of inferiority? Do you feel unloved, unapproved of?

28. Do you have a hard time being consistent in your spiritual life?

29. Is it hard to believe God loves you or approves of you?

30. Do you find it difficult to give and receive love?

If a number of items on this list fit you, you will benefit by soul-healing prayer.

Does Everyone Need Specific Prayer Help?

Everyone's been hurt in life, so everyone's soul needs healing. However, many have already been healed through other means God has used. Remember this statement: *Every experience with Jesus brings inner healing.* What are some healing experiences you've had with Jesus? Here are a few I can think of:

Salvation: If you have accepted Jesus as your Savior, the Holy Spirit has come into your life and joined Himself to your spirit. Your spirit has been completely healed. Also a great deal of soul healing can take place at this time, depending on your openness.

Baptism with water at any age can bring healing to the soul.

At the *release* or *Baptism with the Holy Spirit,* the indwelling Holy Spirit floods the soul and body, filling your speech centers for freedom in praise and witness. Much healing can take place here.[8]

Holy Communion is a time to receive Jesus' forgiveness anew and healing for soul and body.

Confessing your sins and *forgiving others' sins* against you is vitally important for wholeness.

Meditating on Scripture, especially when you receive an individual word just for you (*rhēma* in Greek) can bring great healing.

Through *gifts of the Holy Spirit* such as knowledge, wisdom, prophecy, and so forth, God can speak so directly to encourage, edify, and heal you.

The *fruit of the Holy Spirit,* shown through loving things others do for you, can bring soul healing.

When the Holy Spirit shows you, *who you are in Christ,* your identity in Him, it is healing to your soul.

Other healing experiences for the soul are: *inspired music, dreams* or *visions* given by the Holy Spirit, *witnessing, prayer, praise, worship,* meaningful *sermons* or *teaching,* special *retreats,* and others.

All these experiences can and do heal, but often we have need for further help in order to be as happy and effective as we should.

Yes, the need for healing our souls will continue throughout our lives, for we're living in a world that is still beset by the powers of darkness (Ephesians 6:12). Our own imperfect human natures, and our contact with those who are not walking with God, make it inevitable that we be hurt from time to time. That's why it's important to know how to receive healing from Jesus.

5

Two Important Keys

HE WAS THERE

Father God, in the time span when I was fashioned by Your hand,
You were there and You cared and You loved me.

On the day I was born, Lord Jesus, that first morn,
You were there and You cared and You loved me.

And that very first time I cried, feeling all alone inside,
You were there and You cared and You loved me.

In school I drew a teddy bear, with dark and furry hair,
You were there and You cared and You loved me.

The toy I'd saved for so long, when I came home and it was gone,
You were there and You cared and You loved me.

As the years have come and gone, with so much said and done,
You've been there and You've cared and You've loved me.

There's not one moment of time, precious Lord, in this life of mine,
But You are there, and You care, and You love me.

BETH SHANKS

Before you begin to pray, it's important to have two keys
firmly in hand: *God is unconditional love;* and *God is omnipresent.*

You may have difficulty believing God is unconditionally

loving. You tend to see God as you see your earthly parents, especially as you remember them in childhood. If your father seemed aloof and uncaring, you may see God as not willing to give you the attention you need. You would expect God to say: "Oh, here's Don. I wonder what he wants *now!*" Or "Here's Debbie. What can I say to get her to run along as soon as possible?"

If your parents didn't have enough money, you may see God as not able to provide for you. If your father was weak and sickly, you may see God as someone who cannot be leaned upon or depended on. I prayed with a woman for healing of the memory of her father's death. Until she was healed through prayer, she was afraid to lean on Jesus in time of need because she saw Him as her father had always been—physically weak and sick. If your parents were critical and judgmental, you may see God sentencing you to many days or years of "hard labor," as you try to meet His requirements.

"He'll Never, Never Leave—Unless You Goof"

One day as we were praying with Meg (*see* chapter 1), we were trying to assure her that God would always love her. She nodded her head. "I know," she said, "Jesus says in the Bible 'I will never leave you nor forsake you, as long as you do My will.' "

"Meg," I said, "that's the Scripture the Lord gave you, but do you realize you've added something? Jesus didn't really say, 'I will never leave you as long as you do my will.' That last phrase isn't in the Scripture. I think you unconsciously added it because you're evaluating God's love by the kind of love you received from your parents."

"Well," Meg considered a minute, "I did feel my father would love me only as long as I did everything right. In school, if I didn't make straight *A*s I was severely reprimanded."

"God said He would 'never, never leave you nor forsake you,' period!" [*See* Hebrews 13:5.] Shade explained, "You know now that your dad would not really have thrown you out, or stopped caring for you because you didn't get straight *A*s, don't you? *You* wouldn't leave your children or stop loving them because they brought home poor grades or didn't do their chores properly?"

"Of course not!" Meg replied emphatically. "I see what you mean."

"There's another Scripture," Shade went on. " 'If you then, being imperfect, know how to give good gifts to your children, how much more will your Father in heaven give good things to those who ask Him?' [Matthew 7:11, *paraphrased*]. We tend to think God is not as loving as we are, but He wants to correct this mistake."

"Think of the best earthly father imaginable," I struck in, "and multiply his love by infinity. That'd give you a picture of what God is like. It's hard to imagine that kind of love, even when you've experienced a bit of it. It's so easy to forget or get it out of focus."

An Old Testament Picture

Many people have trouble believing God is love because of what they read in the Old Testament. Some of the descriptions of the way God dealt with people make Him seem unloving.

In the Old Testament, God had not yet been able fully to reveal Himself, nor was it possible in those days for most people to come into any kind of direct relationship with Him. This is why any picture of God in the Old Testament must be brought into line with Jesus Christ in the New Testament. Jesus said, ". . . no one knows who the Son is but the Father, and who the Father is but the Son, and he to whom the Son wills to reveal Him" (Luke 10:22 NKJB-NT). If you want to know what God is really like, you must look at Jesus.

Even so, the great chapter on God's unconditional love, First Corinthians 13, says, "For now we see through a glass, darkly; but then face to face: now I know in part. . . ." (13:12). If *we*, to whom Jesus Christ has been *revealed* and *received,* still see and understand God as if we're looking through dark glasses, how much more was this true of those in the Old Testament?

Do you see the heavenly Father as an unrelenting Judge, and Jesus as the One who loved us enough to die for us? But Jesus Himself says, ". . . he that has seen me has seen the Father . . ." (John 14:9). In other words, "My Father loves you in the same way I do. We think just alike." Jesus said in John 17:26 ". . . The same love the Father has for Me is in you, for I'm in you" (*paraphrased*).

In the liturgy of my own church, when the Gospel is read, everyone stands. When other parts of the Bible are read, everyone sits and listens reverently, but special honor is given to the Gospel records because they contain the words of Jesus Christ. If more people read the Bible with Jesus' words as the focal point, or glass through which they look, they would have a clearer picture of what God the Father is like. Jesus Himself said: "You search the Scriptures for in them you think you have eternal life: but they are they which tell about Me. And you will not come to Me that you may have life" (John 5:39, 40, *paraphrased*).

After His Resurrection Jesus taught two of His disciples how to best study the Scriptures. When He met them on the way to Emmaus, "Beginning at Moses and all the prophets, he expounded unto them in all the scriptures the things concerning himself" (Luke 24:27; *see also* vs. 44, 45).

If you're having trouble with parts of the Old Testament, meditate on passages that show God's love, as when God says to Jeremiah and also to us: ". . . I have loved you with an everlasting love: therefore with lovingkindness have I drawn you" (Jeremiah 31:3). Turn to the New Testament and read such things as, "Behold, what manner of love the Father has bestowed on us, that we should be called children of God! . . ." (1 John 3:1 NKJB-NT). "By this we know love, because He laid down His life for us . . ." (v. 16 NKJB-NT).

Also don't forget that the anger of God in the Bible is not aimed at you, but at the people who steadily refuse to accept His love. He warns them for two reasons: one is that they desperately need Him, and if He cannot win them by His love, He will try to drive them to Him, for their own good. This is like a shepherd and his dog. The shepherd wants to lead the sheep to green pastures and still waters, but if they will not follow him freely, he orders the dog to snap at their heels, to move them in the right direction.

The other reason for God's displeasure is that He will not let the world be dominated and destroyed by evil people indefinitely. There comes a time when the wicked—those who don't want God, who only want their own way, and who therefore fall into the devil's hands, and do his work—must be removed from the scene. The world *is* to be filled with the knowledge of the Lord, as the waters cover the sea.

If you want God, no matter how imperfect you may be, He offers you His unconditional love. The Hebrew word used to describe God's love for His people is *hesed,* which means "loving kindness," a sheer gift, undeserved. It's true for you as it was for Meg. You don't *have to,* and you *can't* earn your heavenly Father's love. He won't take that love away from you. You can turn away from Him, but He will not turn from you.

A Prodigal Father

There was a prosperous farmer in the Midwest who had two children, a girl and a boy. By the time the boy came of age, he was tired of life on the farm and asked his father for the share of the family fortune that would be coming to him. Then he took off for Las Vegas.

He found lots of friends right away. After all, he could buy them drinks, lend them money when they lost at gambling, and throw big parties for them, with lots of wine, women, and song!

He was highly popular for a while, until one night he lost all his money at the roulette table. He didn't even have a few dollars left for food. He asked his "friends" for help, but they treated him as though they didn't know him. Hungry and desperate, he took a job washing dishes in a restaurant.

Months went by as he worked for a bare living. One day, as he was washing dirty dishes, sweat rolling off his forehead, his mind suddenly cleared: "My dad's hired hands are doing better than I am! I've been a silly fool! I'd better head back to the farm. Maybe Dad will at least let me work in the fields." Gathering up his few belongings, he hitchhiked home.

Meanwhile, the father had been waiting for word from his son. Neighbors watching thought the boy had been bad news from the start, and hated to see the father's heart broken.

One day when the father went for his daily walk to the mailbox, hoping against hope that there would be a letter from his son, he saw someone coming down the road. Even though the person was still a long way off, there was something familiar about him—about the way he walked. As he came closer, the father saw his hair and beard were straggly and dirty, and his clothes were in rags—but yes—it was his son! In the father's joy, he ran the distance to meet him, threw his arms around his neck and kissed him. "My son, my son, you've come home!"

The son, stunned at this reception, said, "Dad, be careful! I'm a dirty mess!" And then with a broken voice, "I've been a lousy son . . . I'm not worthy of your love."

"All I care about is that you were lost and now you're home!" said his father, putting his arm around the young man's shoulder, and leading him to the house.

The hired hands came running. "Get ready for a barbecue," the father ordered. "We're going to have a party tonight!" And then to his son, "Go on in and get cleaned up. Your old room is still waiting for you. I even bought a new suit of clothes for you, hoping you'd be home to wear it. It's hanging in the closet. There's some new shoes, too. And, oh, here is something else for you. This ring," the father slipped a handsome gold ring off his finger, and handed it to his son. "It's a family heirloom, you know."

Little sister was looking on, and when she got her father alone, she said "Dad—you've never given me a big celebration like you're giving tonight for my brother! Don't you love me, too?"

"Why, my child!" he replied, putting his arm around her. "You've always been by my side, and everything I have is yours. You know that! Tell me what would make you happy, and we'll do it!"

You probably recognized this story as a modernization of Luke 15:11–32. Dennis says that whereas we call Jesus' parable the "prodigal son," it might well be called the "prodigal father"! The word *prodigal* means lavish or extravagant. The son certainly spent his money extravagantly, but the father was even more extravagant with his love and forgiveness.

Jesus told the original story to show how loving and forgiving the heavenly Father is. It's one of the clearest pictures of our Father's love in the entire Bible. When the son repented and came home, his father welcomed him with unconditional love. There was not even one word of rebuke. God loves you in just that way. He loves you extravagantly—yes—with prodigality!

The Second Key

I flew to Boise, Idaho, several years ago to speak at a luncheon. That morning in the motel I woke up with the word *ubiquitous* on my mind. It seemed a strange word to wake up to, especially since I didn't know what it meant! *Perhaps God is trying to tell me something.* Not having a dictionary handy, I phoned the public library and found *ubiquitous* meant "being everywhere at the same time." Only God could be truly ubiquitous. Can you guess my theme for the talk that day?

The more usual term is "omnipresent." Scripture presents this as one of the basic characteristics of God—*omnipresent*. Omnipresence means being present everywhere, not only in every location in space, but at every point in time. God is present right now in every part of the creation, in the past, present, and future.

Jeremiah realized God's omnipresence when he prophesied, "Am I a God at hand, says the Lord, and not a God afar off? Can any hide himself in secret places that I shall not see him? Do not I fill heaven and earth? says the Lord" (23:23, 24, *paraphrased*).

Consider the psalmist: "Where can I go from Your Spirit? Or where shall I run from Your presence? If I ascend up into heaven, You are there: if I make my bed in hell, You are there. If I fly on the wings of the morning, or dwell in the deepest parts of the sea; even there will Your hand lead me, and Your right hand hold me" (Psalms 139:7–10, *paraphrased*).

Paul, speaking to the Greek "intellectuals" on the Areopagus puts it this way, ". . . [God] is not far from each one of us;

for in Him we live and move and have our being . . ." (Acts 17:27, 28 NKJB-NT).

It isn't just the Father who is omnipresent. What applies to one Person of the Godhead must apply to all Three, for the Trinity is undivided. (*See* John 14:9–20.) It follows then, that our Savior Jesus Christ has been present with us all through our lives, and that He sees us in the past just as clearly as in the present. The Book of Hebrews says we should be "Looking unto Jesus the author and finisher of our faith . . ." (12:2).

People's souls begin to get healed when they realize that Jesus was present with them *throughout their lives.*

When a woman whose husband left her with a large family to raise by herself realized Jesus had been with her all the time through those difficult years, she was healed.

Our friend Beth Shanks prayed for healing from the hurts of a traumatic birth experience and a difficult childhood. She then wrote a poem to express her feelings, which I've put at the head of this chapter.

Soul-healing prayer is not new, but we are presenting some new ways of doing it. For years, there have been many who have prayed for inner healing by asking Jesus "to go back" through the person's life and heal it. What I'm saying here is that it really isn't necessary to ask Jesus to go back, since He was already there. All that is needed is to realize and acknowledge that He was *there.* "In all your ways acknowledge him and he will direct your paths" (Proverbs 3:6, *paraphrased*).

Again, when the Scripture speaks of God's omnipresence, it doesn't mean God stands by, approving the bad things which happen to us and others. Evil came into the world through man's choice to rebel against God. God cannot take away free will from evil men any more than He can from his own children. Through soul-healing prayer we are letting God do for us in our emotions what He wanted to do all the time.

Some Important Differences

Some may say, "I don't see the difference between those who have believed in Jesus Christ as Savior and those who haven't—if God loves both unconditionally and has been with both from their very beginnings!"

It is true that God's unconditional love surrounds every human being all through his or her life, whether they've accepted Him or not. God doesn't want anyone to be lost from Him. But love wouldn't mean anything without free will. God Himself cannot force people to love Him. They must open the doors of their lives to Him voluntarily. He cannot force His way in.

It would be useless to say to someone, "I'll give you a million dollars if you love me!" Or, "If you don't love me, I'll knock you down!" It's no different with God. He cannot force us to love Him; He can only woo us to love Him. Hebrews 9:27 says solemnly: "and as it is appointed unto men once to die, but after this the judgment." Yet I believe that even in the last microseconds of a man's or woman's life, God can speak to him or her. A famous writer of the nineteenth century said Jesus "does not really teach one anything, but by being brought into His presence, one becomes something. And everybody is predestined to His presence. Once at least in this life each man walks with Christ to Emmaus."

An acquaintance was nearly killed in a severe auto accident. She recalls, "I was thrown about twenty feet—literally through the air—and while this was happening, it seemed as though my entire life passed before me." Another person was in a mine cage (the lift that takes the miners down to the workings). The cable broke, and the lift fell to the bottom of the shaft. The lives of those in the cage were saved because they fell through some timbers, which broke the force of their landing. Our friend says, however, "It seemed as though all the scenes of my life were painted on the wall of that mine shaft as we fell!"

The unpardonable sin the Bible speaks of is unpardonable only because the person never chooses to ask pardon, through Jesus. I've had people tell me they had committed the unforgivable sin. My answer was, "Do you want Jesus in your life?"

"Why, yes, of course!"

"Obviously, then, you couldn't have committed such a sin, otherwise you certainly wouldn't want Jesus. Jesus said, 'No man can come to me, except the Father which has sent me draw him . . .' (John 6:44, *paraphrased*). Jesus also said, 'And I, if I be lifted up from the earth, will draw all men unto me' (12:32)."

One young lady I talked to recently told me her grandmother had attended a Christian church for many years but lately joined a non-Christian faith, because their teachings were more positive. In her original church, the preacher's favorite topic was hell and the danger of being lost. He got stuck on this subject and never seemed to go beyond it. I, too, think people have heard enough bad news, and we should emphasize the good. Most people without God realize they're already living in hell; they need to hear good news—a way of escape.

Agnostic Finds Jesus Through Soul Healing

It's important for Christians to realize that Jesus was with them even *before* they accepted Him, and that He can heal the hurts that occurred before they accepted Him. Not only that, a person doesn't have to be a believer in order to get help from Jesus!

Janet, whom I've already introduced, and Cindy Lake, both experienced in soul-healing prayer, were asked to pray with a woman by the name of Jean. She said, "I'm eager for help, but I'm real uncomfortable with Christian terms. If you pray with me, I don't want you to use the name *Jesus,* and I don't want you to quote the Bible. I do, however, believe there's a power outside ourselves which most people would call God."

The prayer partners looked at one another. Was it possible to help a person under those restrictions? Then Cindy replied with Spirit-inspired wisdom, "That's fine, Jean. We'll pray with you. And we won't use the name *Jesus,* or quote the Bible. There's just one thing, though, when we speak of 'that Man,' you'll know who we mean! And if you see Him as you recall the scenes in your life, you can call Him 'that Man,' too. We'll know what *you* mean."

"Well, I can agree to that," she replied.

After Jean told about herself and her early life, they began to pray, and one scene became very clear to her. "I'm about three or four years old," she said, "and my mother is bringing my little sister and me home from the store. My sister is in her stroller, and I'm sucking a popsicle. I need to go to the bathroom, and I don't think I can wait and, oh! I wet my pants! My mom is really angry with me and I feel just terrible."

Cindy suggested, "Now ask 'that Man' to be there with you."

"Okay. Yes, I see Him. He has on a robe that's woven of natural fibers. And, oh . . . !"

At this point Jean began to sob deep sobs. She cried and cried. When she calmed down enough to talk, she explained, "He knelt down right there on the sidewalk and looked straight into my eyes and said, 'You're *not* bad!' A-a-and He put his arm around me, and, oh, I felt such love and acceptance!"

Deeply touched by the tender love of "that Man," Jean wanted to pray again. They agreed to meet in two weeks.

As they settled down to begin, Jean said, "I don't think we were quite finished with the last scene, and if it's all right I'd like to begin there again."

She closed her eyes. "You see," she said, "when we got home, my mother told my dad, and *he* scolded me, so I felt even more ashamed. I remember it so clearly. Would it be all right to pray about it some more?"

Cindy and Janet nodded happily. "This time we'll see what 'that Man' will do about it," said Janet, with a smile. "Just let Him be in control." As they prayed, Jean explained what she saw: "I see Jesus. [In a letter to me, Jean explained, "I'm pretty sure I was calling him Jesus at this session, instead of 'that Man' even though it felt awkward."] He picks me up and sits down in the rocking chair, holding me tenderly. He rocks me—and He doesn't even make me change my clothes first! He doesn't mind that I'm still wet!" She sobbed again with joyful relief.

"It reminds me of that old hymn," Janet said. " 'Just as I am, without one plea / But that Thy blood was shed for me / And that Thou bid'st me come to Thee, O Lamb of God, I come!' "

So it went, and after one or two more meetings, Jean began to really love Jesus. He no longer had to be called "that Man." "But would you please explain to me," she said, "how Jesus can be the same as the God the preacher used to talk about in church? He always sounded as though He was a fierce old man with a long beard, sitting on a throne somewhere up in the clouds!"

Cindy and Janet answered her questions and the one-time agnostic received "that Man" as her Savior, the Lord Jesus Christ.

Soul-healing prayer can bring people into the Kingdom who have been turned off by negative teaching, or bad examples on the part of Christians. Jesus Himself is His own best witness, and when they meet Him and are healed by Him, like the people in New Testament, they "follow Him in the way."

Manifest Presence of Jesus

In soul-healing prayer, God's omnipresence becomes His manifest presence. Jesus is "God in Man made manifest." Jesus said, "He that has My commandments, and keeps them, loves Me: and He that loves Me shall be loved by My Father, and I will love him, and will show Myself to him" (John 14:21, *paraphrased*).

In soul healing we are satisfying the two commandments which Jesus said fulfilled the Law, the Old Testament commands. He told us to love God with all our heart, soul, mind, and strength and our neighbors as ourselves (Mark 12:28–31). We're learning to love God, perhaps, like Jean, for the first time; or, if we already know Him, we're learning to love Him more and more. Because of this, we're learning to accept and love ourselves, and therefore we're able to love those around us more deeply.

While it's true that Jesus can heal you even if you do not yet know or accept Him, it is of utmost importance after you have met Him as your healer, you, like Jean, receive Him as your Savior. Christians not only have God's omnipresence, and manifest presence surrounding their lives, but through the Holy Spirit, they have His indwelling presence. God and His love have surrounded you throughout your life, but if you want this fact to continue on even after this life is over, and if you want really to know Him, you need to make sure you have received Him into your life. Jesus Himself is the key to a joy-filled eternity (Revelation 3:7). And with Him come the keys of His manifest presence and unconditional love—forever.

Prayers: Acceptance and Keeping the Door Open

If you haven't done this, here is an example of a prayer you might use:

> Dear Father, I believe Jesus Christ is Your only-begotten Son. I believe He became a Man, taking on Himself our human nature. I believe He died on the Cross, and poured out His life's blood to clean away the guilt and sin that is separating me from You. I believe that He rose from the dead, physically, and that He can give me a new kind of life.
>
> Lord Jesus, I confess my sins to You—all the wrong things I've done, the darkness, the guilt, and the fear in my life—wash them away with Your precious blood. I accept Your forgiveness. I know that You have cleansed me, and set me free. I invite You to come into my life right now. I receive You as my Savior and Lord. Thank You for giving me the Holy Spirit. I'm a child of the Father! I'm born again of the Spirit! I'm a new creature! Thank You, Jesus!

If you have accepted Jesus, here is a good prayer to use to keep the door of healing open in your life. It is based on a prayer by Doris Smith, a friend with an effective inner-healing ministry:

> God, I want to believe in Your unconditional love for me. It's sometimes hard for me to accept the fact that You love me

so much, but I want to. Teach me to receive Your love and set me free to love others this way.

Father God, I give You permission to go to any level within me, to heal, cleanse, and restore according to Your truth.

To the best of my ability, I invite You to be my Lord unconditionally. I say this because I know You want Your very best for me.

> Thank You, Lord God,
> in Jesus' name.

6

Teach Us to Pray

If people tell you their troubles, or ask you for counsel, or if you have problems or have had hurtful experiences yourself, you need to know how to pray for soul healing. I believe it was the wise and loving Sam Shoemaker who said, "Everyone either has a problem, is a problem, or lives with a problem!"

The disciples said, "Lord, teach us to pray," and Jesus gave them the basic form we call the *Lord's Prayer*. In His parables He taught them it's important to pray persistently, and to expect good things from the Father (Luke 11:1–13). The disciples had heard how He'd prayed and fasted forty days and nights just before His ministry began. They knew He would get up very early in the morning and go out into the desert to pray (Mark 1:35). Sometimes He would pray all night long, as He did before selecting His closest followers (Luke 6:12). They were with Him when He prayed the night before His Crucifixion (Matthew 26:36). Jesus is continuing to open the Word to His present-day disciples, and He's showing us ways to pray we hadn't understood before.

Praying About the Past

We often pray about our present needs or the needs of the future, but what about the *past?* Most would agree with Lady Macbeth: "Things without all remedy, should be without regard; what's done is done."[9] There's obviously nothing to be done about what's past.

For years I had this attitude. I would talk and pray with people and help them with daily concerns, but when it came to past hurts, I would just tell them they "had to forgive." But you know how it is: "I forgive you, but *watch* it next time!" Or, "Now look here! I forgave you when you did this to me last year, and in 1978, but I'm getting a bit fed up with you!" You try to forgive, but when you see the person who offended you, or something else reminds you of the hurt, you get those same old feelings. Like the children of Israel trying to get out of the wilderness, you keep going 'round and 'round the mountain!

The problem was that though you tried to forgive, and prayed to forgive—you hadn't been healed, so you couldn't *forget* the original hurt. It's like a wound in your body. You can cleanse it and dress it, but that won't heal it. The healing comes from a deeper source—the innate restoring ability of the body; but the body must be in good condition in order for the healing to take place. I was right in telling people they should forgive, but I couldn't show them how to do it. I didn't know I could pray for God to heal those past injuries and open the way for real forgiveness.

J. B. Phillips wrote a book called *Your God Is Too Small*, and that's how it was with me. My vision of God was too limited. I didn't know He could reach the past as well as the present and the future. I believe it was Nicholas Berdyaev, the Russian philosopher, who suggested that when Adam fell, he fell into sequential time; that before the Fall, man was not the slave of time. Since God created time, He obviously is not bound by it (Acts 17:26b). Another way to say it is, "God is outside time." This is why, if our faith allows it, He can heal hurts in the past.

"How does God deal with the past?" you may ask. "Will He

put me in a time machine and whisk me back there, à la Buck
Rogers?" God is present throughout all time, but for you, as a
mortal, the "time machine" God uses to return you to past
scenes is your memory. You cannot return physically to the
past, but all the past is recorded in your memory. Through it
God can take you back, so that you see and feel again that
which took place many years ago, this time with the healing
presence of Jesus.

Jesus Gives a Prototype of Soul Healing

I guess I feel especially close to the apostle Peter because I
can identify with his mistakes! It wasn't until I began to pray
for people's soul hurts that I realized how Peter must have
been traumatized by his denial of Jesus. Everyone must have
been talking about it. All four accounts of the Gospel record it,
each with slightly different details. Matthew and Mark record
that Peter "cursed and swore." "When Peter thought about it,
he wept," says Mark. "The Lord turned," says Luke, "and
looked at Peter and he wept bitterly." Luke carries the description of the scene further. He says there was a fire in the
hall, and that Peter was seated by it.[10] John goes into even
more detail. He says, "Now it was cold, and the servants and
guards had lit a charcoal fire and were standing there warming
themselves; so Peter stood there too, warming himself with the
others. . . . As Simon Peter stood there warming himself, someone said to him, 'Aren't you another of his disciples?' He denied it saying, 'I am not'." (John 18:18, 25 JERUSALEM).

Jesus had come to His friends on the evening of Resurrection Day and had shown them He was alive. A week later He
appeared to them again (John 20:19, 20). Following this, Peter

and some of the other disciples went back briefly to their trade of fishing, likely for the very practical purpose of getting some money to live on. We read in John 21 that they fished all night unsuccessfully, and were pulling in to shore, wet, exhausted, discouraged, cold, and hungry. Through the mists of the early morning, they saw a man standing on the beach. He shouted, "Did you catch anything?" and they yelled back, "No!" The man said, "Throw your net in on the other side of the boat!" They did, and now it was so full of fish they couldn't get it aboard, but had to drag it to land. John said to Peter, "It's the Lord!" Peter's reaction was to throw himself into the sea and get to Jesus as fast as he could. Some who aren't so sure "God is love" would have expected Peter to have once again walked on the water, this time, in the opposite direction!

Someone has said, "Jesus loved to give bread and fish dinners." He had fish cooking on a charcoal fire that cold morning, and invited His friends to eat with him. After breakfast, when they were feeling warm and happy and satisfied, sitting by the fire, Jesus began to question Peter.

"Do you love Me?", Jesus asked him three times. Peter had denied his Lord three times, standing by a charcoal fire, warming himself. Now Jesus leads him to affirm his love three times, warmed by a charcoal fire. Jesus is replaying the scene, we may say, so that Peter can be healed, and the charcoal fire is part of the setting. As Peter replied three times, "Yes, Lord, You know I love You," the three denials were healed in his memories. The memory itself would be there as a lesson to be learned from, but the emotional part of the memory was healed by Jesus. Here Jesus gives us a prototype of soul healing.[11]

How does Jesus' dealing with Peter provide a pattern for the healing of your soul? As you pray, Jesus brings back to you what it is He wants to heal. You, the hurting person, visualize the scene as clearly as you can. Perhaps you may remember what you had on, where you were sitting or standing, something you smelled or tasted, and especially what and how you felt. Remember that the memories and emotions are permanently joined together, so revisualizing the scene clearly from your memory will put you in touch with your feelings, so that you can let Jesus heal them.

As you go through the scene the second time, you know Jesus is with you. He was there all the time, but you didn't know it the first time around. Now you're going to acknowledge Him and let Him be Lord. You are practicing His presence in your past. Peter didn't have to "practice the presence" of Jesus because Jesus was there with him physically, as well as spiritually. But Scripture says we today see Him "no longer after the flesh. . ." (2 Corinthians 5:16).

You need to know too that, as one of His sheep, you can expect to hear God's voice. When you pray and share your needs with Jesus, you should expect to hear Him respond. It isn't a one-way street—it's a conversation. In soul-healing prayer we learn to hear and recognize that gentle, inner voice of guidance from Jesus. Peter was able to talk to Jesus directly, but after Jesus' Ascension, Peter had to learn the art of listening, just as you do.

To be healed, you must experience Jesus' unconditional love. Jesus shows us this kind of love in His example with Peter. Peter didn't run away from Jesus in fear. He ran to Him, because he knew what He was like.

After Peter had denied Jesus, Jesus looked at him. I don't believe that was a look of accusation or condemnation. Jesus knew Peter through and through; that's why He was able to tell him beforehand that he was going to deny Him when he was under pressure. I believe Jesus looked at Peter compassionately, inviting him right then and there to look to Him for strength and forgiveness, but Peter wasn't able to receive it at that time. Later, by the lakeside in the early morning, Peter was able to acknowledge Jesus truly as his risen Lord, and be healed and forgiven.

Peter could have been so crippled in soul, psychologically, by the memory of his denial, that rather than waiting with the others in the upper room for the empowering of the Holy Spirit at Pentecost, he might have turned away, and gone back to his former occupation full time. Now, because of Jesus' healing him, he is ready for his next soul-healing experience, receiving the Holy Spirit in power. The fruit of Jesus' healing is clearly seen when Peter stands up, no longer undependable, on the Day of Pentecost, and tells everyone about Jesus so effectively that three thousand are converted that first day (Acts 2:14–41). You can have a soul-healing experience with Jesus that will be just as real as it was for Peter.

Two Kinds of Prayer

You've seen examples of soul-healing prayer with Meg, Jim, Jean, Saint Peter, and others. We can divide soul-healing prayer into two categories. Let's call one *Reliving the scene with Jesus;* and the other, *creative prayer.* Both were experienced by Meg and Jim.

Reliving the scene with Jesus. In the first kind, you revisualize the scene as clearly as possible, acknowledge Jesus' presence, and allow your emotions to be healed. Even the Lord Himself cannot change the past without contradicting Himself, but He can change our reactions to it—our feelings about it.

The key place to begin praying is at the point when you can either visualize Jesus in the scene, or feel His presence—preferably both. In other words, you begin praying where Jesus leads you to begin—where He makes himself known in the picture. It's important to know that with Jesus there, the memory won't hurt as it did the first time. And besides, like a sliver removed from a festering sore, it feels so much better after it's out! And Jesus the Healer is ready to apply His healing salve.

Paul says, "The weapons of our warfare are not made of flesh and blood, but are mighty through God to the pulling down of strongholds; casting down evil imaginations and every high thing that exalts itself against the knowledge of God, and bringing into captivity every thought to the obedience of Christ" (2 Corinthians 10:4, 5, *paraphrased*). Jesus helps us tear down any strongholds of the enemy in the remembered scene; then we invite Him to rebuild on the reclaimed property. Since the memories and emotions are permanently joined together, we need to pray about the actual scene in order to get in touch with real feelings and have them healed. It does not change what happened to us, but it changes our feelings about it, and thus removes its power to hurt us.

An example of this type of prayer is this true account of a student's abduction. With Karine Petersen, a pretty nineteen-year-old, a foreign exchange student from Germany, her real feelings began to emerge without any effort of her own.

While driving with a friend to church, she began to have a flashback to a scene twelve days before, in which she had narrowly escaped being raped. She began to behave strangely, as though she were about to jump out of the car. Phyllis Chandler, the driver, restrained her, and headed for our house.

As the two walked in the door, I started to hug my friend Karine, but she shrank away from me. She didn't seem to want anyone to touch her. Phyllis took me aside and explained what had happened to cause Karine's strange behavior. We sat down in the living room, Karine looking like a frightened animal. Two other friends were there. One of them picked up her guitar, and we sang some choruses about Jesus' love. Gradually Karine relaxed a bit.

The others left, and Karine looked as if she was now ready

to talk. "Karine," I ventured, "Phyllis told me what happened to you a short time ago; the memory's still bothering you isn't it?"

"Yes," she replied in a low, frightened voice. "Since that time it's almost impossible for me to ride in a car, I get so afraid." She showed me how she had scratched the tops of her hands by digging into them with her fingernails.

"What did happen twelve days ago? Can you talk about it?"

With downcast eyes she said, "I was catching a bus on Easter Sunday evening to sing at my church. I'd been waiting some time at the bus stop, and was late already, when a young man drove up and asked if he could give me a ride. He looked nice enough, so I thought, *Why not?* I was tired of waiting out there in the chilly evening air. We drove down the freeway for several miles, then all of a sudden he pulled off, saying he had to stop at someone's house. He turned down a little dirt lane, pulled into a vacant lot, and turned off the motor. I knew I was in trouble. He leaned over and locked the door on my side of the car, then began to struggle with me.

"I was terrified, of course, but I called out at the top of my voice, 'Jesus!' and to my relief the man's hands dropped to his sides. I opened the door, jumped out, and began to run away. Then I realized I had left my purse and camera in the car. The young man still seemed sort of stunned, so I ran back, opened the door, and grabbed my things. He lunged for me but seemed held back by some invisible force."

"Well, we know what that was!" remarked Phyllis.

Karine nodded. "Then I ran as fast as I could to the nearest house," she concluded.

"Praise the Lord! But you know, Karine," I said, "though God did a marvelous job protecting you, your emotions are still in shock. Let's walk back through those scenes, and let Jesus heal your fears." Soul-healing prayer was new to Karine but she was very open. She knew she needed immediate help.

Karine described three scenes: two in the car, and one at the house she ran to, where, after reporting the incident to the authorities, she was interviewed by a policeman. Since the incident with the policeman was the least fearful, we began praying there. This is always a good rule. Start with the least hurting thing; then as the easier scene is healed and faith is built, the person is ready to go on to more difficult ones.

Karine could see Jesus present with her all the way through, except at one point in the car, just before things got rough. "But even there," she said, "there's light on my side of the car, and darkness on the driver's side: I guess that's because I saw Jesus sitting in the backseat, right behind me!"

Suddenly she said, "Oh! After I called out, 'Jesus!' I wondered why Jesus wasn't doing anything. Then I saw a huge man in white, sitting next to my Lord, and holding the wrists of the guy who's trying to attack me, pinning them on his sides. I wonder who it is?"

"Do you think it's one of the Lord's angels?" I asked.

"Oh, yes, it must be!" she replied, tears filling her eyes. "No wonder the fellow couldn't hurt me!" Then as she visualized herself running back to get her belongings, she saw the angel still standing by to protect her.

Phyllis guided Karine to speak forgiveness to her abductor and to pray for his salvation and deliverance. I could see the relief on Karine's face, and felt she'd surely been healed. I reached out my hand to see if she would respond without fear. She grabbed it and squeezed it to say, "Everything's okay"; then gave Phyllis and me great big hugs.

The strongholds of fear the enemy had tried to set up in Karine's life were torn down through prayer, and healing love filled the places where fear had invaded. It was even more obvious she was healed when she consented to tell her story at one of our "Healing of the Whole Person" seminars a few weeks later. She wanted to help others who had been through similar experiences to know they could be healed.

What if the girl had actually been raped? Would we have encouraged her to go back over the whole thing? That's not the way God has led us. It's not likely God would want her to relive that event. Again, we begin revisualizing where Jesus leads us to begin, and we end where He leads us to end. He knows what we can handle, and what would be good for us not to revisualize. When I have prayed with some who have been raped, I find Jesus led them into the scene after the fact, to comfort and heal.

If someone has had a shocking experience, which he hesitates to pray about, you can help him remember a happy scene first, and relive it with Jesus. Then you may be able to move on to the unpleasant memory. For instance, some friends of mine were praying with a man whose grandfather had committed suicide years before. As a boy, he had been the first to find the body. Before praying about the actual event, they led the person to relive a happy time with the grandfather and acknowledge Jesus there.

Creative prayer. In this second type of prayer we are inviting the Holy Spirit to show us brand-new things. First Corinthians 1:28 says, ". . . God has chosen things which don't exist to wipe out of existence things that do" (*paraphrased*). God can create new emotions and wipe out old ones as if they never existed. Also Romans 4:17 says, ". . . God, who gives life to the dead and calls those things which do not exist [such as happiness in childhood] as though they did" (NKJB-NT). If we allow Him, He can quicken (give life to) our dead emotions and give us the love and comfort we never actually received.

Let me give an example of this sort of praying. My friend Janet and I were praying with my husband, Dennis, one day.

(Dennis and I have prayed for one another for various needs ever since we were married.) Though Dennis had been a much-wanted and cared-for child, and although to outward appearance, he had had a sheltered and secure childhood, he actually grew up in a home where there was much insecurity and anxiety. Dennis is an only child. His father was orphaned at an early age, brought up by an older sister. His mother's father had died while she was still a child. His mother was a fine person, highly intelligent, but a very tense and anxious person, and as far back as Dennis can remember, she was severely handicapped by rheumatoid arthritis. His father was a minister, unable to give much time or attention to Dennis. Dennis's father was a good man in every sense of the word, but probably due to his own deprivation of a father figure, was not able to convey to Dennis much sense of what it means to be fathered.

The family moved to the USA from England when Dennis was nine. This meant that both Dennis and his father were coping at the same time with a good deal of "culture shock." The father could not help Dennis adjust to the new country, because he himself was having difficulty adjusting. Because of all these factors, there was a general air of anxiety hanging over the family. Added to this, while in England, Dennis attended an old-fashioned English day school, which was only one step removed from the days of Charles Dickens!

"As I looked back to my childhood," says Dennis, "it seemed gloomy and threatening. I didn't want to recall it."

Since Dennis did not want to think back into his childhood, and since in any case there was no definite event for him to pray about, he just had a general feeling about it, we took a different tack. We suggested that Dennis remember something that he liked to do when a child, and let Jesus build around it.

"I liked to draw," said Dennis, "and I can see myself drawing pictures with a friend. We're about age eight. We liked to draw machinery, gears, steam engines, trains, and other mechanical things. We're sitting at the kitchen table, drawing with pencils, and having a good time."

I suggested that Dennis invite Jesus to be there with them. "Oh," he said, "yes, Jesus is there. He has some paper and He's drawing too!"

"What kind of picture is Jesus drawing?" Janet asked. In his visualization, Dennis looked at Jesus' paper. "It's a colored picture. He's using crayons. He's made a background of green mountains, and there's trees with brown trunks. There's a river in the foreground." I was amazed at how clearly Dennis seemed to be seeing all this. It was obvious the Holy Spirit was at work. "The sun is just coming up," he went on. "In the foreground is a bird. It looks like a penguin walking by the water; no, it's a duck; no—it's a *goose!* Oh, it's a wild goose and it's beginning to fly! Now all of a sudden the room we're drawing in is lit up with bright sunshine."

"What does it all mean?" I asked.

Dennis paused a moment, then replied, "I guess He's trying to tell me that although there was darkness in those early days, it wasn't the threatening cloudiness before a storm, it was the darkness before the sun comes up. The sun is coming up, and like that wild goose, I'm going to fly high and far in the sunshine!"

It doesn't sound very dramatic, does it? Yet Dennis testifies, "In that one simple piece of visualization, Jesus was able to change my whole basic feeling not only about my childhood, but about life in general! Because of the gloom hanging over my childhood, I viewed life basically with anxiety about what was coming next. The future was always vaguely threatening. In a way that I cannot explain, Jesus conveyed to me that my childhood was a time of promise, and that the future held, not threatening things, but good things."

Dennis accepted Jesus when he was eleven, and when he was forty-one, he experienced a further release of the Holy Spirit. He went on to become an internationally recognized leader in church renewal, yet he still needed soul healing for his childhood memories!

When the Holy Spirit had freedom, his soul was filled with light and joy, but often the hurts of the past would keep this from happening. He says "I *know* that visualization was guided by the Holy Spirit. It really changed my feeling about life, and I haven't lost it."

This kind of prayer, in which we allow the Holy Spirit to inspire our creative imagination, can help in many ways. In it, He can create a brand-new memory, or He can create new scenes within an old memory.

With Meg and Jim, God led us to use both kinds of prayer—sometimes interchangeably.

Your Creative Imagination

Some folks object to this kind of praying because, they say, it's just "imagining something that didn't really happen, and what's the good of that?" Please note that I'm *not* asking you just to use your imagination; I'm inviting you to let the Holy Spirit inspire your imagination. The visualizations that come are so creative you will know they are from the Holy Spirit.

In Dennis's case, he used his imagination to choose the scene from his memory. He had often sat and drawn pictures like that with his friend George. However, as soon as the Lord was invited to come into that picture, the Holy Spirit began to take command and inspire Dennis to see things that he himself could not have imagined.

The Lord can in this way heal an actual event that is recalled. Dr. Robert Frost gives a good example in his book *Set*

My Spirit Free.[12] A young woman had been plagued for years by nightmares. The Holy Spirit helped her to recall that when she was four or five, a tramp had broken into the house, and when he realized he was about to be discovered, had come into her bedroom and hidden under her bed. The man was caught, but even though she was physically unharmed, her soul was deeply scarred with fear. As she was prayed with for soul healing, she saw Jesus in the scene. He looked under the bed, and then He and the little girl called the parents and asked them to set the best dishes out, because a special guest, the tramp, was coming to dinner! Jesus did not change the past event, but He gave the young woman a new picture of it, as He would like to have had it happen; this healed her emotions, her feelings about the real event. Her fears vanished. The nightmares were healed.

Was it scriptural? Jesus was actually there, that was a fact. What she saw Jesus do was like pictures of Him in the Scriptures. He takes our fears away; He treats forgiven sinners like kings and queens, if they will let Him; and He often did important things at the dinner table! "No, God doesn't change history," I once heard John Sandford say, "but if allowed, He changes the way we interpret our own history."[13]

Seeing by Faith

Some are turned off by the term *imagination*. It sounds to them like something unreal, as we say, "a figment of the imagination." It seems to be playing into the world's hands, because the world regards the Christian faith in general as imaginary. Realizing this problem, I suggest a more scriptural term, "seeing by faith," instead of "imagination." Faith is having eyes to see the invisible.

Read the eleventh chapter of Hebrews. Enoch saw by faith

the possibility of being caught up to God. By faith Abraham left his home and looked for a city he didn't know existed. Verse thirteen says of the many people listed in this chapter: "These all died in faith, not having received the promises, but having seen them afar off, were persuaded of them, and embraced them. . . ." By faith they saw a new picture, they visualized it, and moved into what they saw.

There's a balance to be considered here. In seeing by faith, what we see must be in accord with God's Word and God's loving nature. It's highly important to know the Scripture, or be praying with someone who does, in order to keep from getting off the track.

Whatever terminology you use, God has given us the ability to "see by faith." The enemy likes to pose semantic problems to keep us from the very help we need. Don't worry over terms, but ask God to use your creative mind for Him.

Three Steps to Release

Forgiving is essential to the soul-healing process, because we cannot truly be free until we have forgiven.

If we are followers of Jesus, we know we *must want and will to forgive everyone and anyone who has wronged us.* This is the first step. Unless we forgive, we cannot receive God's forgiveness, nor will we be open for healing. Unless we "will" to forgive, we cannot claim the protection of Christ's cleansing blood as we pray.

If we are being honest, though, we will recognize there are times when we forgive with the will, but cannot forgive from our emotions. "I forgive you, but I'm going to stay out of your way!" "I forgive you, but you'd better not do it again!" With some situations, we have to say, "Lord, I don't *want* to forgive him—not after all he's done to me!" That's all right, that's honest. The Lord will say to you, "Do you want to want to for-give him?" "Yes, Lord, because You want me to, I want to want to!" This is good, and God accepts it.

For some, the second step of *being healed in their memories* happens spontaneously, but most need specific help and prayer.

As our souls are healed, we can go on to a far deeper level of forgiveness. The third step is to *forgive again, seeing yourself at the age you were when the hurt occurred.* Through Jesus, speak to the person just as though you were there. The recording tape of your memory has been rolled back to the past scene, and in effect you *are* there.

Shade O'Driscoll was the first person to bring this to my at-tention. We had prayed with a woman for healing. I then en-couraged her to forgive the one who had hurt her. She did so but there was no outward evidence that it meant anything to her. Then Shade said, "Now let's do it again, seeing yourself at the age you were when the hurt occurred." As the woman spoke forgiveness in that way, she began to weep. I realized from this that forgiving, first-person present-tense, as from the original scene, could touch the emotions, and therefore the subconscious in a way I hadn't known before.

There will be further detail on these three steps as we go along.

7

Your Hurt Child of the Past

You are a product of all your yesterdays. You respond today according to how you were treated as a child, and the attitudes and opinions your parents instilled in you. The foundation was laid during the first five or six years of your life. Little children's emotions and attitudes still rule the lives of multitudes of adults, unless something has been done to change the early patterns.

Through soul-healing prayer, you can allow God to give what you needed but missed in childhood. The first few years are especially important.

My friend Doris Smith, mentioned earlier, points out some helpful facts about children's formative years, which she derived from reading the works of Robert J. Havighurst, University of Chicago, and the late Dr. Erik Erikson, Harvard psychologist:

In the first mental year (not necessarily only the first chronological year), you learned to trust, to hold yourself open to another human being, to develop an intimate relationship with another person. If this isn't digested into the emotions, you aren't ready for the next step.

The second mental year you learned independence. You were beginning to sort yourself out from your mother's identity. It was the proper sort of independence; you were beginning to develop your own ego (in the right sense of the word). If you heard *no* too many times, and realized your decisions didn't carry much weight, you may not have fully developed at this level.

In the third mental year (could include ages three to five) you learned initiative, that is, knowing how to step out on your own. You weren't afraid to learn about and try new things.

As most people know, the first five years are most significant in forming basic emotional responses and concepts of right and wrong, says Doris.

Your inner child has all the feelings built up by contact with parents and environment before you were old enough to evaluate and process what was happening to you. He or she is dominated by feelings, reactions to what is received through the senses, even though not understood. "Children usually pick up, before the age of six, the emotional 'feeling tones' of one or both parents," says Dr. Cecil Osborne, author and counselor.[14]

Some Christians think psychology, the study of the mind and behavior, is a naughty word, and I'm cautious about what I accept in this field, too. As with anything, such information can be beneficial or detrimental. When I find a truth which is clearly stated in Scripture several times, and not in opposition to what Jesus or the apostles taught, in my opinion it's worth considering.[15]

Understanding about your inner child can give you further handles to help your soul be healed, and help you help others, too. It seems to me there are two inner children: the Hurt Child and the Creative Child. In this chapter we'll look at the Hurt Child.

The Hurt Child

Dr. Osborne says further, "There is nothing seriously wrong with any of us except 'hurts,' usually experienced in childhood."[16] Hurts in childhood go deeper than grown-up hurts, because you were not able to defend yourself and therefore were highly vulnerable. Verbally you were no match for adults. And you couldn't hop into your car and speed away from the problem; your foot wasn't able to reach the gas pedal!

Those injured in childhood's first six years will usually need more prayer help than those blest people who can say, "I was truly loved by both my mother and my father. There isn't a time in my childhood when I didn't feel loved." This is the greatest gift a parent can give a child. Most of us, however, can't say that. When people haven't received needed love and respect in childhood, there's a little child inside who's never been allowed to grow up. When Jesus says, "Let the little children come to Me, don't hold them back," we can hear Him speaking about that Hurt Child locked into your past. You can let this emotionally damaged child within come to Jesus for healing, even though you are now an adult.

Healing the Child Within

"I can testify to the beauty and power of inner healing," says Joyce,[17] a young lady who shared her story at one of our seminars. "In the spring of last year I moved, changed jobs, and was divorced all in the same week! The result was a breakdown in September of that year. Personal stress, coupled with professional stress, had brought me to the verge of suicide." Joyce went on with her story:

I was taken to the hospital in a withdrawn state. A beautiful woman I worked with came to see me. She whispered something about Jesus in my ear. All I can remember was "When you think no one in the world loves you—God loves you." How beautiful that sounded! The next morning when I awoke and then was discharged, this woman invited me to her home and within hours led me to Jesus Christ.

In the months that followed, prayer and walking closely with Jesus was the note of every waking moment. He sent me to my family in another state to tell them I loved them, but that I needed to be released to live my own life. Then He showed me the basis of my fear of failure, my professional drive for success. He taught me to trust. But the most special healing was when He taught me to love.

I was praying one evening on a rock ledge overlooking the city. I saw Jesus, myself, as I am now, and myself as a child. Jesus said of the child, "There are happenings in her memories that make this little girl hurt. If she will embrace and love Me, I will take that pain away." So I encouraged my inner child to go to Him. But she was like an iceberg. She wouldn't move or smile.

I began to cry and ask Jesus what was so bad in her past that she couldn't even love Jesus.

He said, "If you will love Me as you are now, she will love Me."

So I embraced Him. As I looked around, tears began to roll down her cheeks; her lips began to quiver. She ran to Him and there we were, big me, and little me, both crying and being embraced and loved by Jesus!

Suddenly my whole heart took on a new warmth. It was like God passed His hand through it. Since that day I have been able to love my friends and family in a deeper way than I ever felt possible.

"A Little Child Shall Lead You"

All of us know it's important to be reconciled to family and friends, but somehow we haven't always realized that there may need to be a reconciliation between our adult-self and child-self.

During soul-healing prayer, one man saw Jesus sitting in a local park waiting for him to come and talk with Him. As he walked up to Jesus, he saw a child with Him, and upon coming closer, realized it was himself.

He didn't want to go to Jesus because the child was sitting

there, and he didn't like himself when a child. Now he began to feel sympathy for the seven-year-old sitting with Jesus in the park. Jesus asked him to give the boy a hug; and as he did so, the man began to cry. He had begun to accept his child-self. Do you realize how much you need to do this in order to be a whole person? Your past self is part of what you are today, and if you reject it, you are rejecting an important part of yourself.

Using a little child for an example, Jesus said, "Whoever receives this little child in My name receives Me . . ." (Luke 9:48 NKJB-NT). So as we receive that little inner child that we used to be, we also receive Jesus' healing for those inner needs of the past.

Some people dislike themselves as children so much, it's difficult for them to pray about their childhood. The man we've just spoken of would say, "I don't want to think about my childhood at all. The memories are too depressing. I can't stand that little child!" This attitude revealed how much he needed healing. If you feel this way about your child-self, it will help to realize that Jesus was there with you in your childhood. You cannot reject yourself as a child without rejecting Him, too, in that part of your life, because He loves that child.

The prophet Isaiah said, ". . . a little child shall lead them" (11:6). If you have a Hurt Child within, I believe it's vitally important to find and face that little child—the part of you which has been ignored, rejected, and despised. Let your hurting little child put its hand in Jesus' hand and together you'll find the way. If you let him or her be healed, your little child, guided by Jesus, can lead you to being a whole person.

If your inner child is not allowed to be itself, but is deeply rejected, all kinds of strange behavior may occur. People who greatly dislike themselves in childhood are those with self-identity problems. Others may not actively dislike or hate their inner child, but still have hurts and bad memories that need to be healed.

Beginnings Are Important

A distraught father brought his son to Jesus for healing. The boy was being tormented by a demonic spirit, which was causing him to have violent seizures. The first question Jesus asked was, "How long has this been happening to him?" The father said, "From childhood" (Mark 9:21 NKJB-NT). To get to the root of a problem we, like Jesus may need to ask, "When did it begin?" Even with a problem that is clearly demonic, it is important to know, if possible, how and when the evil spirit got control, so you can cast it out, and keep it from getting in again by the same route.

Satan is sometimes called the "enemy of the soul," and that's a good name, because the soul is his favorite point of attack. He builds hurtful or abnormal patterns of behavior as early in our lives as he can. Then he can simply manipulate these patterns when he wants to get us into trouble.

Beginnings are very important. It's sort of like loading a ship. Everything is loaded on before it leaves the dock, and that cargo stays with the ship wherever it goes on the voyage.

For many years Jackie[18] had been looking for a woman to mother her. Mistreated at home, she had run away at fourteen and lived in various foster homes, while she searched for someone to take her mother's place. She met Jesus, and was baptized in the Holy Spirit, and began to pray for soul healing. One night the person praying with her asked, "Jackie, when did you first decide to reject your mother?"

"I . . . I guess it was when I was six years old," Jackie answered hesitantly, "and brought home a report card with a *C* in Conduct. My mother beat me 'til I was black and blue and locked me in my room. I was afraid to tell my father, for fear mother would beat me again."

Jackie described her prayer time like this: "It was like stripping a wall which had many layers of wallpaper on it. Those layers were made up of a lot of people and scenes I didn't want to look at or remember."

The Inner Child in Scripture

The first Scripture I found on the subject of the inner child was First Corinthians 13:11, "When I was a child, I spoke as a child, I understood as a child, I thought as a child; but when I became [an adult], I put away childish things" (NKJB-NT).

In the context, Paul is appealing to the Christians in Corinth to "shape up" and stop being what we today would call "denominational," competing among themselves. They were playing around with God's supernatural gifts, too, instead of using them to bless the Church and the world.

Paul is saying: "My friends, please grow up! All these wonderful things are not going to benefit you unless you love one another."

We can take Paul's words in a slightly different way, though, and this is the way I saw it one day. When you were a child, it was okay to speak, think, and act as a child. It really is all right to be a child when you *are* a child! It's not only all right, but it's very important. In fact if you didn't have a chance to enjoy your childhood, you may have grown up with many regrets and deficiencies.

The oldest child of many children, who has been forced to grow up too soon, may feel as if he or she was forced to be a parent prematurely. An only child who doesn't have other children to relate to, may become so precociously adult that other children reject him.

If a parent so much wants a child to excel in sports that he or she doesn't allow the youngster to play games just for fun, but makes him spend hours and hours in strenuous practice, that child may be injured. "Stage mothers" who force their children into theater may do the same. The child may become a success, yet hate every moment of it, both as a child and as an adult. A father who wanted to be a concert musician, or a medical doctor, but for various reasons couldn't, may push his child into an unsought for career to satisfy *his* ego. The "child evangelist" may so bitterly reject what was done to him by his parents and others who promoted his precocity, that he will reject them and everything they believe in, because he was forced to play the role of a little adult, and not allowed a normal childhood.

Adults Should Not Be Childish

". . . but," Paul goes on in First Corinthians 13, "When I became an adult, I put away childish things . . ." When an adult begins to act like a hurt child, that is "childish" behavior.

Because of hurts in childhood, some people have been stopped in their growth. A man who is thirty years old, and still acts as if he were three, may succeed in a business or profession because his self-centered childish drive makes everyone afraid to oppose him; but he isn't likely to be successful in personal relationships, especially in marriage. A three-year-old racing down the driveway in his coaster wagon is cute, but when at thirty he races down the highway in his high-powered car, childishly disregarding the law, and risking his own and other people's lives, it is cute no longer.

The two-year-old who throws her teddy bear across the room, or her spoon on the floor because she doesn't get what she wants, is tolerated; but if her behavior goes unchecked to the point that as a woman of thirty-two she throws the toaster against the wall, or a dish at her husband's head, it isn't funny anymore.

A friend of mine is married to a very fine man who has had a problem with temper. One day his wife made what seemed to her a very mild criticism of something he had done, but he was furious! He yelled, he nearly kicked a hole in the door, he threw things. As his wife stood and watched, one part of her thought: *I've had enough of this. Why should I put up with it?* But her spirit said: "You know you care deeply for him—that's why you married him! You were sent to help him be all God intended him to be."

Fortunately, the wife had been listening to some tapes on soul healing and reading some books on the subject. In one of the books she read: "If someone overreacts, it shows an area where they need healing."

Well, she thought to herself, *this is an overreaction for sure.* Typically, her husband calmed down rather soon and began to feel very much ashamed of himself.

"Honey," said the wife, "if I said something to offend you, I'm truly sorry. Please forgive me? I do love you, you know."

"Of course," said the husband, looking very downcast. "It was such a silly little thing. Why would I act like that? I just don't know why I got so upset," he went on, "I'm really sorry, but I just can't seem to help it. I sure do feel like an idiot. It's a wonder you or God have anything to do with me. That's sure no way for a Spirit-filled Christian to act." They sat down on the couch together.

"What did I say that upset you so much?"

"I heard you blaming me. I feel I've been blamed all my life, one way or the other."

"You know, honey," the wife responded, "I'm really glad this happened, because your overreaction shows where we can begin to pray. Tell me where in the past you've felt blamed."

As they talked together about it, the man realized that his father had never really given him approval for anything he did, but had usually been critical. He realized that his mother had herself been a very guilt-ridden person. More subtly, it emerged that his mother had become ill shortly after his birth, and there was strong reason to believe he felt responsible and guilty about that. His violent reaction to his wife's minor offense was from anger bottled up against his father, and against others who had criticized him.

He could never remember expressing anger to his father, and if he had expressed anger on the job he would have been fired. The only safe way to express his anger was at his poor wife!

Over a period of time, the man and wife prayed about the memories, letting Jesus come and heal. There was no instant cure, but the temper tantrums became gradually less frequent, and much milder. Not only that, but the man began to regain a freedom in the Spirit that he seemed to have lost for many years. Soul-healing prayer works!

The wife also realized from this experience that she had a tendency from childhood to blame others. This was the result of having had siblings who often tried to blame *her,* so the only safe way was to shift the blame as quickly as possible!

Both temper tantrums and blaming others are immature Hurt Child manifestations. A person tries to control by temper because he or she feels unable to handle matters any other way, and blaming others seems the best way to protect oneself.

Why not simply pray for deliverance from the bad temper? There are times when deliverance is necessary, when there is a real spiritual oppression that needs to be broken. I'll say more about this in a later chapter. Many times though, we think problems are demonic when they are only the manifestations of a hurt soul. And if deliverance prayer is needed, but isn't backed up by healing, it won't last. Healing closes the doors by which the enemy has been able to get in, and rips out the equipment by which he has been able to manipulate. It tears down the carefully planned stronghold he had built in the victim's soul. The enemy won't be able to hang around for long, if there is healing and forgiveness.

How a Little Child Behaves

In the previous example, the husband was regressing back to childish behavior because he could not cope with life at an adult level. He had been hurt as a child, and that unhealed hurt in childhood had kept him from becoming an adult in that area.

It's helpful to remember just how a little child behaves. Remember what it was like when you were a child, or when you were raising your own children? How does a child act when angry? He or she may pout, whine in a high-pitched voice, throw temper tantrums, kick the door, or the wall, or the cat, or what-have-you; he or she is ruled by feelings. He or she may cling to a teddy bear or a blanket as a security object. If things get really tough, a child's very common reaction is "I'll run away—then you'll be sorry!" and many small children have actually tried to put this into practice.

For a child, every problem is huge. He is either laughing or crying. Life is great, or life is terrible. He cannot yet look ahead and see that troubles don't last forever.

So the grown-up person, when he or she regresses into the Hurt Child, may speak with a little childish whiny voice; may be shy about speaking in public, may shed tears to get his or her way; may want to run from problems—may actually use what Alcoholics Anonymous calls the "geographic cure": "I'll just go somewhere else and start over; then everything will be okay!"

Like the child, the "Hurt Child" adult is self-centered, and wants constant attention. Every problem that comes along is a major catastrophe: "All is lost!" He or she tries to avoid responsibilities, and may cling to another person for security.

The Hurt Child in Marriage

Have you had a friend or acquaintance, who, after years of seemingly happy marriage, suddenly leaves spouse and children, and goes off with someone else, just as if the original family had never existed?

A really lovely woman left her devoted husband and five beautiful children for another man some years younger than herself. All the family are devoted Christians, and highly active in their church.

When this happened, I had not yet become aware of "soul healing," but looking back, I realize now that this woman was regressing into her Hurt Child. A person may be "Spirit-filled," but if Jesus hasn't been allowed to heal the hurts of the past, that person may still be highly vulnerable to such temptation. Somewhere along the line—I don't know her history—this woman had been hurt in a way that made her unable to cope with being an adult. She couldn't handle the responsibilities of caring for her family. Therefore, she went back to being a child. When she was a child, the world revolved around *her,* and now she still wanted to be the center of attention. She decided to run away. Her paramour was as immature as she was, so, like two little children, they ran away, ignoring all responsibility, all consequences.

This is not to excuse the woman's behavior, but it certainly helps to understand it. Seeing where a problem comes from helps us know how to pray with or for others with similar

temptations so their lives—and perhaps their marriages—can
be saved and healed.

Did Jeremiah Need His Soul Healed?

We often think of Bible people as if they were perfect, and
had no problems. It's unfortunate, because a wonderful thing
about the Bible is that it's honest about the people in it. The
bad is not hidden, but brought out so that we can see those involved were human beings like ourselves, with similar problems.

One day, reading the first chapter of Jeremiah, I realized
that he felt very inadequate. When God called him, notice
Jeremiah's response:

> Then the word of the Lord came to me, saying, "Before I
> formed you in the womb, I knew you; and before you were
> born, I set you apart, and ordained you a prophet to the na-
> tions."

> Then I said, "Ah, Lord God! Look, I cannot speak: for I am a
> child." [Jeremiah was probably a young man when his call
> came from God.][19]

> But the Lord said to me, "Say not, 'I am a child': for you shall
> go to all I shall send you, and whatever I command you, you
> shall speak. Don't be afraid of their faces, for *I am with you,* to
> deliver you," says the Lord.

> Jeremiah 1:4–8, *paraphrased*

Even after Jeremiah is told by God Himself the important
plan He has for his life, Jeremiah responds with something
like, "I'm too inferior and inadequate to do the job, Lord.
You've got the wrong person!"

Why would a young man like Jeremiah feel like a child,

unable to speak in public? The experiences Jeremiah had in his formative years, could have made him respond to God as he did. Nevertheless, Jeremiah wisely is honest with God and tells Him how he feels. To put it in modern terms, "he got in touch with his feelings."

God told Jeremiah in so many words not to live in his Hurt Child but to rise up to the level of His Spirit. God's word, the *rhēma,* to Jeremiah brought him a new kind of wholeness. To His newly called prophet God says, in effect: "You will speak the words I give you. You are to trust completely in Me and My ability in you. Don't be intimidated by the looks on men's faces." (Have you ever been nervous about the look on people's faces? I have.)

Best of all, God tells Jeremiah "I will be with you," and that brings healing and confidence. God has told you and me the same thing. When you *know* God is with you, you can do anything He calls you to. You can be sure God is going to do everything possible to help you, just as He did Jeremiah.

Jeremiah received soul healing through admitting his needs and fears, accepting God's living Word to him by faith, and by being aware of God's continuing presence with him. We do all these things as we pray for our souls to be healed.

The Same Pattern With Moses

The patriarch Moses gives us an even clearer example. When God called him, Moses' reply was much the same as Jeremiah's. His whole response to God at first is negative: "Who am I, that I should go to Pharaoh . . ." (Exodus 3:11). ". . . when I come to the children of Israel, and say to them, The God of your fathers has sent me to you; and they shall say to me, What is his name? what shall I say to them?" (v. 13). ". . . Look, Lord, they will not believe me, nor listen to my voice: they'll say, The Lord did not appear to you" (4:1). ". . . I am not eloquent . . . but I am slow of speech, and of a slow tongue" (4:10, *paraphrased*).

It's small wonder the Lord gave in to Moses and said, "All right. I'll let Aaron be your spokesman!" (*See* 4:14–16.)

Notice the Lord's response to each of Moses' objections is, in effect, "I will be with you. I will put words in your mouth." Much later on, when Moses is about to lead the people on from Sinai, we still see his continued lack of confidence. "You've told me to bring up this people, but You haven't told me whom You're going to send with me!" (33:12, *paraphrased*). And God's answer again is "My Presence will go with you, and I will give you rest" (v. 14, *paraphrased*). Moses' hesitancy is also seen in Numbers 10:29–32, when he pleads with his brother-in-law, Hobab, to go with them as a guide in the wilderness, just as though God had not promised to lead them with the pillar of cloud and pillar of fire!

Why would the mighty Moses be like this? Do we have a direct clue in that we do know something of Moses' infancy and childhood? He was taken from his mother at birth and left alone in a cradle of reeds, floating in the river. How long was he there? He was reunited to his mother for a time, and then taken by the princess as an adopted son. What a lot of hurts could have been caused by all this!

Some of the Hurts a Child Experiences

What are some of the hurts you may want to pray about from your childhood and youth? Were you:

Embarrassed or severely punished by parents for childish "sexual investigation"?

Lost, or locked in a closet or other enclosure for a time?

Bitten by an animal?

Exposed to harmful sexual experiences: molestation, incest, or other similar traumatic experiences?

Rejected by a parent, or sibling, or not affirmed by one or both parents?

Shocked by divorce of parents?

Hurt by the death of parents or parent figures, death of grandparents, siblings, or other close family members?

Seriously ill, with extended bedrest or hospitalization?

Frightened or upset on the first day at school?

Sent away to school, far from home, at an early age?

Embarrassed by teachers, in front of the class?

A failure in school?

Transplanted to another country during childhood or teens?

Brought up by an alcoholic parent?

Hurt by your father's leaving for war, or business for a long time?

Put into an adult role too soon?

Suffering from a physical handicap or learning disability?

Beaten by parents, or beaten and harrassed by bullies at school or play?

Teenage years Were you:

At the beginning of puberty, not given information by parents on sexuality, or given wrong parental teaching about sexuality?

Embarrassed by parents for revealing intimate details to others?

Privacy of self and belongings not respected?

Not accepted on your first date?

Rejected by your first love?

In an accident, saw one, or caused one?

Overweight and embarrassed by comments about it?

Molested in some way?

Though you are a product of all your yesterdays, if you allow God to heal you, He can change things so that your yesterdays no longer control your todays. And God will be the blessed Controller of *all* your days.

Prayer: Reliving the Scene With Jesus

As you have been reading these chapters, perhaps you have remembered some hurtful actions or occurrences in your past. *If they are too painful,* you should have some people you feel confident in pray with you. If that's not possible, read the next chapter, and the prayer at the end of it. Then come back to this one later, as the Holy Spirit leads you.

Find a quiet place to pray. Take the phone off the hook! Reread some of the Scriptures given previously on God's unconditional love and omnipresence. He accepts you just as you are.

Think about God's love for you. He is perfect love. There are no conditions on His love for you. No one man or angel, circumstance or mistake, can separate you from His love for you. "God is love." There are no strings attached to His love. You don't have to be "perfect" to be loved by Jesus. (Pause here.)

Get comfortable, close your eyes, and ask Jesus to guide you. Put your eyes on Jesus; He is your healer. If you can't visualize Him, accept that He's there by faith. Sense His presence with you now. Ask God to bring a specific scene to your memory for healing. (Pause.) Now, with Jesus with you in whatever way you can experience Him, let Him lead you into the scene *at the point He indicates,* and let Him walk with you through the hurts. It won't hurt as it did the first time because you're acknowledging Jesus' presence with you. Allow His love to move into every part of your being: spirit, soul, and body. (Pause here awhile.)

In Scripture Jesus allowed the children to come to Him and He laid His hands upon them and blessed them. Allow Jesus to bless you, as a child or as an adult, with His love. Tell Him how you feel, pour out your needs, then be still and listen to what He says to you. He hurts when you hurt. He knows what it is to suffer. As it says in Isaiah 53, "by His stripes you are healed." He took your pains upon Himself. Let Him tell you about it, and how He's going to help you be relieved from your suffering. Receive the new insights and understanding He gives you. (Take some time to pray right now.)

Receive a new love for your own inner child. "I accept you, my child-self, and allow you to be healed and live. I will no longer reject you; I accept you." Let Jesus give you a deepened love for others, and especially for God.

Put down your book for a while, and pray further. (Pause here.)

Speak forgiveness: At the end of your prayer, forgive the person or persons involved in the hurts you have recalled with Jesus, and that He has been healing. Do this, visualizing yourself at the age you were when the hurt occurred.

Here's a sample of how to pray: "Through Jesus, I forgive you [name the person]. I will no longer hold this against you or judge you for it. I set you free and set myself free. Jesus has healed me." (You can edit this prayer to suit the situation.)

If the person you need to forgive has since died, pray in this way: "Jesus, will You please tell [name the person] these words: '[Mom or Dad or other] I forgive you. You did the best you knew how. Jesus is setting me free to forgive everyone. Jesus has healed me. I love you.'"

(We are careful not to seem to speak directly to a person who is no longer alive, even though in the scene you're recalling they were alive. The above sample prayer is to avoid any suspicion of attempting to communicate directly with the departed, which is, of course, strictly against God's rules (Deuteronomy 18:10, 11; 1 Samuel 28:7–20). We can't determine where a person has gone after this life, but in giving Jesus the message, He will take care of those details.)

Now, thank God for what He's done, and remember that He is with you at all times. Practice His presence daily, moment by moment.

8

Your Creative Inner Child

SOME CHILDREN SEE HIM

Some children see Him lily white,
The baby Jesus born this night,
Some children see Him lily white,
    With tresses soft and fair.
Some children see Him bronzed and brown,
The Lord of heaven to earth come down;
Some children see Him bronzed and brown,
    With dark and heavy hair.

Some children see Him almond-eyed,
This Saviour whom we kneel beside,
Some children see Him almond-eyed,
    With skin of yellow hue.
Some children see Him dark as they,
Sweet Mary's Son, to whom we pray;
Some children see Him dark as they,
    And ah! they love Him, too!

The children in each different place
    Will see the baby Jesus' face
Like theirs, but bright with heavenly grace,
    And filled with holy light.
O lay aside each earthly thing,
And with thy heart as offering,

Come worship now the infant King,
'Tis love that's born tonight!

WIHLA HUTSON

SOME CHILDREN SEE HIM
Lyrics by Wihla Hutson: Music by Alfred Burt
TRO—© Copyright 1954 and 1957 Hollis Music,
Inc., New York, N.Y.
Used by Permission.

Look at a well-loved little child if you want to see what the Kingdom of God is like. Dena Cousins is my brother Bob's first grandchild. She is a beautiful little girl of three, and how Grandpa and Grandma Reed love her! All the family tease Bob about how he dotes on his granddaughter. Dena's love for her grandpa is pure and open. She loves to run and jump into his arms. She trusts him and is confident in him. She knows he thinks she's wonderful, and around him her little face lights up more radiantly than ever. There's lots of laughter around when grandpa and granddaughter are together.

Dena is getting a good beginning in life. She's always been loved, by parents and grandparents, so she'll have lots of love to give. She isn't getting treatment that would later cause her to be unkind, aloof, neurotic.

Jesus calls us to this open, happy, free kind of life. When He wanted to show what the Kingdom of heaven is like He "called a little child to Him, and set him in the midst of them" (*see* Matthew 18:1–6). He sets honest, trusting children who love Him openly in our midst and says in essence, "I want you to be like this. It's the happiest way for you to live. Without child-likeness you won't enter into My Kingdom" (Mark 10:15, *paraphrased*).

Childlike or Childish?

"But wait a minute," you may say, "in the last chapter you were telling us not to be living back in the child. Now you say Jesus told us to be like children. Which is right?"

There's a vast difference between being child*ish* and being child*like*. We quoted Paul's appeal to the Corinthians to "grow up." He said something similar to the people at Ephesus: ". . . we should no longer be children, tossed to and fro and carried about with every wind of doctrine . . ." Ephesians 4:14 (NKJB-NT). The adult who *acts* from the Creative Child, open, happy, and free, is child*like*. The one who *reacts* from the Hurt Child, as in the previous chapter, is child*ish*. The more the Hurt Child is healed, the more the Creative Child can emerge and develop. Wholeness of your inner child brings wholeness to you.

Dennis says, "Some people pride themselves on their maturity, when it's really just middle-age spread!" As we get older, we tend to get rigid and stuffy. Perhaps *we* need to set a child in our midst and say, "Teach us to be happy and open, like you!" You may say, "There are so many troubles in the world, I don't have a right to be happy!" Or, "My work is so important and I'm so busy. I don't have *time* to be happy!"

God didn't create us to do tasks, but to have fellowship with Him and one another. The "tasks" came in after we fell away from God. As we get back in touch with Him, even our work is supposed to become joyful, because He's working with us. If you took yourself less seriously, you'd probably do better work. And everybody needs to take time off, just to play once in a while.

"But," you may say, "I've forgotten how to be childlike." Ask Jesus; He will show you. You have some friends who are free. Spend time with them and be refreshed. Father William Sherwood is a retired Episcopal priest, and at ninety-one, is one of the most continually joyful people I know. He's not afraid to clap his hands with glee, give a friend a big hug, or even dance with joy. I think that's one of the reasons he has lived so long; he's so free and open.

In the charismatic renewal of the church, there is a freedom in praise and worship that releases the inner child. There's clapping hands and lifting them in praise; there's singing and praying spontaneously in the Spirit; there's taking time to love your neighbor; yes, sometimes there's even dancing. Musical dance groups, such as Merv and Merla Watson's, and Amanda Smith's (she does liturgical choreography) have led the way in bringing dancing as praise to God back into the Church. If you're not sure how you would feel in a setting of such freedom, just try it in small portions, until you can adjust to the whole meal!

Maybe you're not ready for freedom in praise; there are other ways to minister to your inner child. One thing my husband, Dennis, has done for me is to read me some of the children's books I missed when a child. In those post-depression days, my father was forced to spend long hours on his job, just to support the family. He loved to read out loud, too, but time didn't often permit it. My mother, for financial reasons, was unable to complete her schooling. She was an intelligent woman, but I don't think she ever felt adequate, or knew what to read to us. So it is Dennis who is feeding my Creative Child!

He's read to me the *Pooh* stories of A. A. Milne; C. S. Lewis's *Chronicles of Narnia,* Kenneth Grahame's *Wind in the Willows, Stuart Little* by E. B. White, to name a few. We've also read other works that are a combination of childlike creativity and mature wisdom, such as Richard Adams's *Watership Down,* J. R. Tolkien's *Fellowship of the Ring* and C. S. Lewis's *Space Trilogy.*

Games are important to the Creative Child. In my youth, our family rarely played games together. Everybody seemed to be off "doing their own thing." (I do remember playing *Monopoly* and tiddlywinks on some occasions.) In the religious circle in which I was brought up, to play cards was considered wicked, I suppose because some people misused them. (I often wondered why cards were preached against, while constructive advice, for kids who were spending their time necking in parked cars was not given from the pulpit. It seemed the very kids who often got in trouble being off by themselves, would have had a better start in life if they'd been given some positive guidance in their recreation, including wholesome games.)

So again, Dennis and the Bennett family have helped me learn to enjoy games. When Dennis and I were married, games were the furthest thing from my mind. After all, being a Christian is serious business, and hadn't I "put away childish things"? But I learned from Dennis that game playing is a form of relaxation and fellowship, and (low be it spoken) it could help keep the "gray matter" active! He pointed out to me that Saint Teresa of Avila, that wonderful lady who loved God so much, was reportedly very fond of playing chess! We are busy, and happily so, in the Lord's work, but every now and then we take time to have fellowship around a game (although Dennis still hasn't succeeded in convincing me it would be fun to learn to play chess. Apologies to Saint Teresa and all other chess players!)

How Children See It

Please don't get the impression that soul healing is only concerned with the hurts of the child. I'll be talking later about the healing of hurts sustained in adult life. Our earliest days, however, are the foundation upon which everything else is built, and that's why healing for this time of life is so important.

Shirley Fawdrey, a friend of ours who was studying educational psychology, says this:

> Our long-term memory is like a library. The main problem is not one of storage but of retrieval. In early life, children code their memories in pictures, since they are creative and also don't have a developed verbal capacity. But we adults code our memories verbally, and can't remember some early events because we don't have the right card catalogue. In soul healing Jesus gives us the right catalogue card, or the picture of the early event, so it can be retrieved and relived with Him.

Children think in pictures; adults think in words and concepts. It's obvious, then, why it's sometimes difficult to know why we're hurting inside, and how to get to the problem. After all, as adults we've also "put away childish pictures." The pictures which are revealed to us in prayer are like library cards presented to the Librarian (the Holy Spirit) who brings up a book which had been lost in the basement of the library. Now the hurtful emotion can be dealt with.

Sometimes as we're praying with a person about childhood, he or she will say, "I see a picture which doesn't make any sense. It really seems silly to tell you about it." Then my prayer partner or I will say, "That's great! Often the ones which don't seem to make sense, make the most sense. Tell us about it!" Some of the insights the Lord gives at these times reach and heal the deepest.

A small child normally thinks and visualizes creatively. These abilities are in Christians and non-Christians alike, and they should not be stifled as we grow up, although they often are. In school, perhaps you were told to draw a tree. Your tree was purple with orange bark! If your teacher was a creative person, your effort was accepted, but the chances are you were told, "That's not right! Look at little Johnny's tree. It's green with brown bark; *that's* what trees should look like," and so your creative originality begins to be squashed.

Those who haven't been squelched in their creativity are the ones who excel in the fields of space travel, computer technology, communications, cooking, art, writing, music, and so forth. They are the Shakespeares, the Rembrandts, the Einsteins, the Edisons, the Madam Curies, the Admiral Byrds, the Christina Rosettis. Dr. Cecil Osborne says:

> Studies have shown that at the age of five nearly all children measure high on creativity, imagination, and spontaneity. By age seven, only 10 percent of the same children score high on creativity. Among adults, only 2 percent rate high on creativity, imagination, and spontaneity. The conclusion of researchers is that these emotional responses have been stifled by criticism and fear of failure induced by rejecting adults. Some of it, of course, is the result of unconscious imitation of adults who pass on to children their emotionally starved personalities.[20]

God wants to bless your creativity and increase it! If you have Jesus functioning through your spirit, soul, and body, you should excel in every way, because you have both natural and supernatural ability.

Seeing Jesus

A little boy was drawing a picture. His mother came to look and said, "Son, what are you drawing?" "Aw, Mom, can't you see? I'm drawing a picture of God." "But," she replied, "no one knows what God looks like!" The little boy, unabashed, replied, "Well, when I get through with this, they will!"

We all visualize a little differently. When we pray and encourage a person to visualize Jesus, the accuracy of the picture isn't important. What's important is that they're seeking by faith to be more aware of His healing presence. It's true that "we see Him no longer after the flesh," that is, through human eyes on earth, but there's nothing wrong with seeing Him "after the Spirit." After Jesus' Resurrection He looked so different in His glorified Body that Mary Magdalene mistook Him for the gardener. It was the loving way He said her name *Mary* that caused her to know Him.

My brother Dr. Robert H. Reed, a dental surgeon in Tampa (the proud grandpa I told you about), had a vision of Jesus one night. The Lord appeared as very athletic, bursting with energy. I think Jesus appeared that way because Bob, who has always excelled in sports, would be able to identify with Him better. When a friend of Janet Biggart's visualized Jesus in soul-healing prayer, she saw Jesus in modern clothes, dressed in a T-shirt and jeans! She questioned in her heart why He was dressed that way, rather than in more biblical-looking attire. She felt His answer was, "You've seen me as the Lord of long ago, but I want you to know I'm Lord of the here and now also."

Many have been inspired by the painting above the altar in Holy Innocent's Episcopal Church, Maui, in the Hawaiian Islands. It's by Delos Blackmar, and shows Jesus and His mother as Polynesians. In Saint Matthew's Church, Fairbanks, Alaska, a stained-glass window portrays the Holy Family as Indians, with the Wise Men bringing appropriate gifts of skins, ivory, and so forth. The beautiful carol *Jesous Ahatonhia* ("Jesus Is Born"), written in the Huron language by Saint Jean deBrébeuf around 1643, puts it into words:

> Within a lodge of broken bark
> The tender Babe was found,
> A ragged robe of rabbit skin
> Enwrapped his beauty round. . . .
> The chiefs from far before him knelt
> With gifts of fox and beaver pelt.
> Jesus your King is born, Jesus is born,
> *In excelsis gloria.*[21]

At the beginning of this chapter I gave the words to the Hutson-Burt carol "Some Children See Him." Is it important—or is it even okay—to wonder what Jesus looked like, and to try to visualize Him? Is this just trying to keep on seeing Him "after the flesh"?

There are many evidences right in this present day and time that Jesus is not against showing us His appearance. People do have visions of Him. I told how He appeared once to my brother Bob. One Sunday morning, coming out of church, one of Dennis's friends stopped him. "I saw Jesus in church this morning," he said excitedly. "He was standing behind you at the altar rail!" Perhaps you know of other examples.

In the spring of 1981, Dennis and I held a healing mission in Christ Episcopal Church in Denver, Colorado. There in the children's classroom on six very plain-looking windowpanes, there appeared a picture of a man, first noticed six or seven years ago. The face was seen first, and is more clear than the rest; now the whole body can be seen faintly. In a photograph, the entire person can be seen quite clearly. It looks like Jesus as we usually imagine Him. The Denver *Post* did an article on it and sent a glazier out to see how the picture got there, but he could offer no logical explanation. Someone else tried scraping or sanding the window but could not remove the picture, because it is somehow imprinted in the glass at different depths. The church has not tried to gain a lot of publicity about this, but it is very impressive to see. If this is a miraculous picture of Christ, as the rector, Father Dave Wilson and others feel, then it's interesting he chose to appear in the most unpretentious spot—a children's classroom! Was He reminding us of something?

Then there's the Shroud of Turin. It is well publicized that the Shroud is believed by many to be the actual burial cloth which covered the body of Jesus. In some way, a picture of Him was imprinted on the cloth (many believe by a burst of radiation when His Body was glorified by the power of the Holy Spirit at the time of His Resurrection). The picture was only seen in its full detail ". . . when in 1898 a lawyer, Secondo Pia, an amateur photographer, after many unsuccessful attempts, managed to get an imprint on two glass plates by using a cumbersome Voigtlander camera. . . . Those stains on the Shroud were actually a life-size photographic negative. When reversed by photography, they revealed a positive portrait of Christ!"[22]

Even before the image on the Shroud of Turin was clearly seen through photographic means, it's believed that many of the famous old world painters were inspired by and based their paintings on it, beginning as far back as the fifth century.[23]

If it's wrong for Christians to try to visualize Jesus, then the great painters of Christ's likeness: Titian, Constable, El Greco, Michelangelo, Raphael, Rembrandt, Van Dyck, Guercino, and scores of others, including the various modern artists who have tried to portray the Lord, have seriously erred. In that case, all those beautiful stained-glass windows would "have to go," as well as paintings and photographs!

Jesus used our visual ability when He spoke to us in parables. He talked of everyday things like: gardening, farming, eating, marriage, animals, people, forgiving. He gave us clear pictures, so we could remember what He said. If Jesus were here in His actual glorified body today, He would probably use television as one way to reach us, because He knows how much we are influenced by pictures. He should know. He created us!

First Chronicles 16:11 says: "Seek the Lord and his strength, seek his face continually." "Anybody who receives my commandments and keeps them will be one who loves me; and anybody who loves me will be loved by my father, and I shall love him and show myself to him" (John 14:21 JERUSALEM).

I'm not saying it's necessary to visualize Jesus in order to receive healing for your soul, but it is a great help. We know faith is assisted by hearing, but also find it is assisted by seeing.[24] You were able to visualize easily in your childhood. The ability must still be there; it just needs to be released.

"I had a good beginning," Pam[25] shared with Janet and me. "My parents were what you would call ideal. Then, about the time I entered my teens, they began to have trouble because my father thought he was in love with another woman. Every night I'd hear my mother crying, asking my father why he couldn't love her. My older brother began to behave wildly, acting out his distress. Our family was a mess for a whole year. Then my father got his life straightened up, and we came back to normal."

This terrible year might not have been so damaging to Pam if the family had not always been so happy and normal. The contrast before and during the crisis was so extreme, it left a deep scar. We led Pam in creative prayer, and as we prayed, Jesus telescoped a year into about forty-five minutes! Jesus and Pam went for walks, played on the swings, laughed and talked, and did the usual things children enjoy. He wiped away the tears of that year with His presence and love.

In creative prayer, Jesus shows us what He, if allowed,

would have done in our lives to help us, and actually lets us experience it now with Him in our emotions. He changes the history of the heart.

A Man Child

One day when reading Revelation 12:5, I noticed Jesus was called the "man child." I know this is just the King James Version's old-fashioned way of saying "male child," but the Holy Spirit sometimes takes liberties with literal meanings, and He broadened this one for me. *Man child*—how could a person be a mature man, and a little child at the same time? Then I realized just how true this is of Jesus!

Ephesians, chapter four, says Jesus is the ultimate goal of maturity:

> Till we all come, in the unity of the faith and of the knowledge of the Son of God, to be completed adults, so that we measure up to what Christ is in His fulness: that from here on we are no longer like children [hurt children], tossed back and forth, and influenced by every idea that comes along, by the tricks of men, and the sneaky cleverness through which they are waiting to deceive us; but speaking the truth in love, may grow up into Him in all things, which is the head, even Christ . . .

> 4:13–15, *paraphrased*

"The measure of the stature of the fulness of Christ," is our goal. The balance comes in when we realize that Jesus, who is the greatest example of maturity, at the same time maintained a childlike simplicity of obedience and faith. Jesus said, "I do what My Father tells Me. I do nothing of Myself." No one else had ever turned water into wine, fed multitudes with a tiny amount of food, walked on water, but Jesus did. He was able to do these things because of His childlike simplicity and obedience to His Father. Though fully mature, He had the faith and openness of a little child.

One thing is clear: God seems to be able to do His mighty works where there is childlikeness. It is our pride and false maturity that squelches them.

It's significant to note that Paul in Ephesians 4 does not say we are to "grow up" in the way we normally use that phrase. To us, "grow up" means that some day we're going to be "grown up"—we will have arrived! The word Paul uses in Greek is *auxesomen,* which is from *auxo* or *auxano* meaning simply "to grow." Paul says we are to "grow" into Jesus. I believe we'll be growing all the way through this life. The thought excites me. The Reverend John Powell says, "In the garden of humanity what is not growing is dying."[26] Being childlike doesn't spoil our ability to grow, but keeps us from taking ourselves too seriously.

I believe the fully integrated person is capable of being a Maturing Adult and a Creative Child at the same time. The two are complementary. As Jesus Christ was both perfect Man and perfect Child, so we should grow into maturity while living in childlike simplicity.

You need to learn how to allow your Creative Child to be expressed spontaneously. (I'm not talking about adults *involuntarily* regressing to childhood; that would indicate deep problems.) Try to overcome the thinking which has divorced the Creative Child from the adult in you. This will happen more and more as you love your inner self.

The Creative Child is: loving, open, happy, spontaneous, unaffected, trusting, affectionate, honest, responsive, straightforward, imaginative, emotionally free. The Creative Child learns easily and laughs easily. When inspired by the Holy Spirit, the Creative Child happily praises God, sings and prays in the Spirit, lifts and claps hands, dances before the Lord. Be willing for God to make you open in many of these ways.

Faith is assisted by seeing as well as hearing. As you pray this week, practice seeing Jesus by faith, and sense His love for you. Know that God is with you at all times. Practice His presence daily, moment by moment. He said, "I will never leave you" (Hebrews 13:5).

Prayer: A Creative Prayer for You

You may want to try praying this way. Right now take the phone off the hook and move to a quiet place, where you aren't likely to be disturbed.

Begin by thinking of yourself as a child, elementary school age. Most of us can remember something about those years. Where did you live and how did you feel then?

Think of a place where you liked to be alone, where you felt safe and happy in your childhood. It could be your own room, the kitchen, at church, on the farm. Perhaps it was in your backyard, in the park, in a tree house, at a fishing hole, a lake or pond, a special vacation spot. Try to remember what you looked like and what you were wearing. Let yourself feel some of the happy feelings you had then. If you can't remember a happy scene, let Jesus create one for you. Settle in this scene and pause.

Even if you didn't know Jesus personally in those days, He was with you just the same. By faith try to visualize Him there. See Him as your favorite artist pictures Him if you like. You may see Him in biblical dress or modern, or just see Him in silhouette. You may not see Him, but sense His presence. You may feel His hand on yours, or on your shoulder. Is He to your right or left, in front of you or behind, or even above? Allow Jesus to make Himself known to you. Let Him be to you what you needed most. (Pause here for a while.)

Jesus brings peace and joy. He loves you with total love. He accepts you just as you are. He knows every imperfection, yet He loves you as if you were the only person in the world. He really enjoys being with you. If there's something you want to tell Him, do so. *Listen.* There might be something He wants to say to you.

Lay this book aside. Get comfortable, close your eyes. Spend some time with Him right now.

9

Parents Are Important

TO MOTHER ON MOTHER'S DAY

Contemplate and try to while the hours away,
Hours that make days; days—weeks; weeks—months.
But that in a minimum of time, I could see you all.
Far away, too far, too earthly far,
Still here, but far,
Here on earth, but not to be reached. . . .

Oh, that I could run, run home, out into our kitchen
And—and—find Mother there.
Pies in the oven, sweet-lined sugary dishes here and there,
Bobby eating the first little cakes to come from the oven.
Two sweet little girls trying to help,
But being slightly in the way.

What's missing?
Though our busyness puts those thoughts aside,
A missing presence is not here.

Let me run to that kitchen,
Don't hold me back!
Let me, let me—but that I could. . . .

To lie on the floor and weep at your feet,
To feel your comforting presence,
Your hands cool upon my brow.
To lie at the feet of the *one* with whom
I said my first good-night prayers.

Ah! Are there tear stains on this page?
I'm sorry, but times come when all emotion seeps out,
And one falters humbly and weeps.
Weeps for the want of the one
Whose heavenly presence is *so* greatly needed.

And, Mother dear, *forgive me please* for words
Spoken at unhappy times or strained moments,
When I temporarily forgot to show my love.
Mother, for almost as God, I love you.

WILLIAM STANDISH REED[27]

Mother, for almost as God, I love you. Those are strong words. A mother seems almost omniscient to a child, especially during the first six years, and some of that feeling may remain on into early adult life, as this poem, written by my brother Bill, movingly shows.

Before birth your mother was certainly the more influential of your two parents. You depended totally on her. She was a key part of the creative process that gave you life. Not only your physical but your psychological entity was engulfed in hers.

After birth, your mother held and fed you, and you continued to feel very close to her. By eighteen months, you were beginning to distinguish yourself apart from her, but you still looked to her for your feelings of goodness and worth.

Mothers are important. They are the "*home*-makers"; that is, they are the ones who make home, home. They have to be "all things to all people." They are counselors, child psychologists, mother confessors, cooks, cleaning women, nurses, seamstresses, bakers, interior decorators, chauffeurs, cheerleaders, bank tellers, florists, gardeners—you name it! Mothering stretches a person.[28]

To be psychologically whole you need to have had a good relationship with your mother, but that doesn't always happen. Mothers aren't perfect. They don't always show wisdom or love. It would be great if each of us had had a completely loving, fully understanding mother to give us a good start in life.

One Reason for Suicide

It is highly important for the small child to see his or her mother as good and loving. Dr. Charles Mangham, a child psychoanalyst, says: "When a child is one or two, he automatically and unconsciously recognizes his own extreme helplessness. . . . He endows his mother with omnipotence, so he no longer has to feel frightened and helpless in what to him is a hostile world. The belief is cast in stone. Any time it is shattered, he is going to feel helpless, as he did when he was small."[29]

Because of the need to see mother as totally good and reliable, if she falls off her pedestal, it can be devastating to the young person. I have, on a number of occasions, asked depressed, suicidal individuals, "When did your mother disillusion you?" Often he or she will remember the time quite well; then we can pray about the past scene, and defuse the bomb which was ready to detonate.

My friend Shade O'Driscoll sometimes asks God the Holy Spirit to show the person what his or her mother was like when *she* was a child. The Lord can reveal such things, even though we have a minimum of actual facts. Seeing what happened in the mother's life to make her into the kind of person she is can bring both compassion for her, and insight too. Somehow it's easier to forgive a little child than an adult.

Can you remember a memory of a happy time you had with your mother? Relive this memory with Jesus, and let God emphasize the good there was. After you've prayed this way, try praising God for your mother each day for several weeks. (Do the same with your father, too.)

Left by the Side of the Road

God often uses conferences to bring matters that need healing to the surface. I was speaking for an Aglow retreat on the West Coast. At the close of one of the morning sessions, we were happily enjoying God's presence, singing the song, "Turn Your Eyes Upon Jesus." I found afterwards that one woman had left the meeting in great distress.

I went to her cabin, and she answered the door, her eyes red from crying. We sat down. "Maxine," I asked, "would you mind telling me what has upset you so much?"

"Well, Rita," she said, a little hesitantly, "as we were singing that song, I saw Jesus coming towards me from a distance, but as He came closer, He came to me, then went right by without paying any attention to me. I don't understand why."

"Hm-m. I can certainly see why you would be upset," I replied. "Tell me, what happened to you early in life which made you feel greatly rejected?"

Maxine looked down sadly. "When I was three, my mother left my little two-year-old brother and me in the snow, by the side of the road. She was an alcoholic and didn't know what to do with us. We were found in time, and taken to some relatives who cared for us, until we were adopted several years later."

I felt like weeping as she told me this, and I took her hand. "Maxine, there's no question about the deep hurt you suffered there," I said. "But tell me about your adoption. Do you remember anything from your childhood with your adoptive parents?"

"Yes, I remember one thing vividly," she replied. "I was so

happy to have a home of my own and parents of my own. One day I ran in to my new mother and said: 'Mom, I'm so glad you and Dad adopted me. I'm so happy for my own room, and my toys. I love you!'

"Her reply was a great shock when she said, 'Well, *I* don't love *you*. It's your father who wanted you!' I was utterly crushed. Once again I had been rejected by a mother."

I sat for a moment or two, taking in what this second rejection must have meant to Maxine. Then I said gently, "Which memory would you say hurts you the most: your natural mother's leaving you by the side of the road, or your adoptive mother's rejection?"

"Definitely my adoptive mother's words hurt the most, as I recall them. I can understand why my alcoholic mother did what she did. She probably didn't even know what she was doing. But I just don't understand why my adoptive mother would have treated me like that. That's what hurts the most."

I asked Maxine to recall that scene so many years before in her adoptive home. She could clearly see the dining-room table, and her mother, and best of all, she saw Jesus. She saw Him coming over to her. He stooped down and said: "Though your father and mother forsake you, I will take you up" (*see* Psalms 27:10).

And that's just what He did. He picked up little Maxine in His arms and comforted her. Tears began to flow again, as God touched and healed the emotions in her memory. After a while I helped her offer forgiveness through Jesus to her adoptive mother.

When Maxine saw Jesus come to her and then seem to pass her by, she interpreted it to mean He had rejected her. This had actually happened with her adoptive father. He wanted to adopt the child. He came to her. But because of his wife's feelings, to keep peace in the home, he had to keep his relationship with his little daughter at a distance. In essence, *he passed her by*.

Understanding brings healing. God used this picture to show Maxine what had happened to her, and also to bring the two of us together to pray. Jesus can be to us whatever we need, so He gave her His love to meet the void of her parents' love.

I later got in touch with Maxine by telephone, three years after our meeting together in 1978. She said, "You don't know how much that prayer meant. It's been a turning point in my life. I've grown so much, and I have a deepened understanding of others.

"Recently my mother went through some serious surgery, and she asked me to forgive her for not being a real mother to me. I realize now she couldn't have. She first needed to be healed so she could love herself; then she would have had the ability to love others. Our relationship and openness with one another is so much better. God's blessing is like a snowball—it gathers more and more people into it as it goes along!" Maxine also said she understood now that Jesus wasn't really passing her by. She interpreted it that way because of her hurt and rejection. "If I had looked into His heart, I would have understood that, as He passed by, He was calling me to follow Him," she said.

Mary, the Most Perfect Mother

Those who haven't had a good mother experience would do well to consider Mary, the mother of Jesus Christ, the model of perfect motherhood.

When I was a teenager, several times I visited Christ the King Roman Catholic Church for mass on Christmas Eve with two of my school friends in Tampa. Being Protestant, I didn't understand all that was happening in the service, but came away feeling that women were respected there because of the honored place given to Mary. Other churches I attended taught about what the apostles and other great men did, but there wasn't much said about women. They often seemed ignored.

Teaching about Mary in Christianity as a whole seems to be a matter of "feast or famine." In some parts of the Christian community, she is highly honored, while in other parts, she seems to be ignored. This is too bad, because Mary is a very important person. Eastern Orthodoxy speaks of her as the "first Christian," since she was the first to bring Jesus, the Incarnation of God, into the world, as each believer is supposed to do. Saint Paul says to the Galatians, "My little children, for whom I labor in birth again until Christ is formed in you" (4:19 NKJB-NT). What greater distinction could any human being have than to be chosen as the mother of Jesus Christ? Any person feeling the need of "mothering" can hardly do better than look to Mary as a primary example—the most wonderful of all mothers.

Remember how Mary wrapped Jesus in His blanket and laid Him in the manger? As she fed Him, she held Him close to her heart. Mary and Joseph must have walked in total agreement; otherwise they couldn't have moved so fast to escape when Jesus' life was threatened at the age of two. She readily accepted the revelation from God given to Joseph about moving the household.

She took care of Jesus, comforted Him when He needed it, made sure He got enough rest, fed Him well and did all the things a mother does. Tradition says the robe for which the soldiers were gambling before the Cross was woven by Mary for her Son. John tells us it was "without seam, woven from the top throughout" (John 19:23)—surely a labor of love. She was with Him through His worst trial, and her faith in Him continued to and through His death. The disciples, except for John, all "forsook him, and fled" (Mark 14:50), but Mary had the inner stamina to stay with her Son through His cruel death (John 19:26).

We don't have much record of her words, but what we do have is highly significant. Her instructions to the servants at the marriage feast in John 2:5 (*paraphrased*): "Whatever he says to you, do it," sums up her attitude about her Son. The rest of the time Mary seems to be quietly observing, and "kept all these sayings in her heart" (Luke 2:51).[30] Mary had wisdom when not to share the things she knew. She often just held them in her heart and talked only to her heavenly Father about them. Take the time right now to thank God for Mary.

Fathers Are Important, Too

When you were a child, your father was important to you in a way that you may never have thought. He was a prototype of God to you. You drew your picture of what your Father in heaven was like from your father on earth. Since this is so, it is doubly important to have your relationship with him healed. If you haven't, it may have kept you from being open to God at all; or may have saddled you with a false idea of God that distorts your whole approach to Him.

For self-identity, the father is most important to the boy, and the mother to the girl, but for a picture of God and relationship with Him, the earthly father is most important to both male and female. Proverbs 17:6 says, ". . . A child's glory is his father" (TLB), or ". . . the glory of children is their fathers" (AMPLIFIED). So another *basic key* in soul healing is to be healed in your relationship to your earthly father, forgiving him for hurts he caused you. This can make you more open to God.

When a father leaves during the first five years of a child's life, especially if his leaving is permanent, due to divorce or death, the child may be devastated, unless someone uses great wisdom. The child goes through a number of feelings: *Perhaps it's my fault; my dad doesn't love me; my mother's to blame;* or, *why did God let this happen?*

While Dennis and I were speaking at a conference in Canada in 1978, a man suddenly realized the grief he had been carrying since he was eight years old because of his father's death. Prior to this, he hadn't realized just how important his father had been to him. When we broke into small groups, he was prayed for, and tears began to pour down his face.

He reported to the conference, "Today was the first time I have cried in forty years!"

A little child doesn't understand death, and may not realize the deceased parent didn't want to leave. So a feeling of rejection may come into a child's life at this time.

At a meeting in Oregon, David, a fine-looking man, came up to say he had been healed of a similar hurt. "Just a short while ago," he said, "as you were telling about the healing of the man in Canada, the Holy Spirit reminded me of some long-forgotten memories of resentment and bitterness because I was kept from attending my own father's funeral, when I was ten years old. I was able to bring the Lord into that situation, ask forgiveness for resentment toward the family, and receive cleansing and healing."

A letter from friends of ours, Dick and Carol Greenwood, tells a similar story. Dick is a certified public accountant. His wife, Carol, says, "After three nights of reading your book *Trinity of Man,* Dick awoke at four A.M. and found himself weeping after a startling dream about his father."[31]

Carol recalls, "Dick was shocked by the sudden death of his father twenty years ago. He was an only child, and he and his father were good companions. The family was close, but tended to avoid outward emotional expression. Dick, who says he never dreams of people he knows (he's an elephant chaser, big-time adventure dreamer!), was amazed that in his dream he was able to release the grief so long suppressed. [So many men are taught by word and example to hold back their tears when children, it's no wonder they have trouble expressing them as adults.]

"Since this breakthrough, Dick is suddenly free to pray out loud with me daily," says Carol, "and this comes after twenty-two years of marriage! He had not read a great deal about soul healing, but was absolutely convinced of it after the release he experienced."

An attractive woman with two children, still toddlers, came to church seeking counsel after her husband had left her the week before. She was particularly concerned about her four-year-old boy, who was waking up in the middle of the night, distressed and vomiting. Talking with her, I discovered there was a grandfather the boy loved very much.

"Tell the child," I advised, " 'Daddy loves you but he will be gone for a while. You know Grandaddy loves you, too, and will be like a daddy to you.' Ask the grandfather to let the little fellow spend as much time as possible with him for a while—that isn't usually too hard for grandpas to do!" I concluded, with a smile.

The mother responded, "That's interesting. My boy has been asking me if he could spend the night with Grandpa, but I didn't know if it was the right thing to do!"

Next to the father, the grandfather is most important for the child's picture of God and for a little boy's self-identity. (Grandmother is next to mother in importance for the girl in her self-identity.)

Different Kinds of Fathers

There are two essential gifts a father can give to his family: one, to love his wife; and two, to give physical and verbal affection to his children. A child needs to know he's a delight to his father, and shouldn't feel he has to earn his approval. If a child doesn't feel approved of by his father or mother, throughout his life he may feel compelled to win approval from others.

One man told me after a seminar, "I broke up my marriage when my son was fairly young, and did a number of things I'm not proud of. I didn't realize until today that I was such an influence to lead my child to or away from God. Perhaps my son doesn't believe in God now, because he doesn't believe in me, and has rejected me. I'm going to write him today and ask him to forgive me for any way I've hindered him."

The father who is notoriously difficult to live with is often easier to forgive than the "nice" but indifferent father who is so damaged himself, he has no human affection to impart. It's easy to see that the cruel, drunken, or brutal father will need to be forgiven, but the "nice" father has supposedly done no wrong, so the child seems to have no grounds for being angry with him. But the child *is* angry with his father—angry for being ignored—for lack of affection and interest. With no point for release of his anger, he may repress it, or not even know it's there. Repressed anger and hate take a longer time to be recognized.

The Rev. William Vaswig tells the facts preceding his son's healing from mental illness: ". . . because I was a pastor, my children saw me not as an ordinary father, but as God's representative. This was especially true of Philip, because he was extremely sensitive. Instead of telling me to 'go to hell' as other teenagers might have done, Philip kept all his anger within. . . .

In communicating God to people, I had communicated to our children a God whose representative I had become, and one whom they surely were in no position to rebel against. How do you talk back to a powerful father when God stands directly behind him? Even if it is perfectly justifiable, even if he is wrong, do you dare talk back to a man who represents God?"[32]

Ministers pack a double wallop as omniscient fathers to their children, and to a lesser degree to the children in their congregations. Their influence is great.

Some Questions to Ask

If a person is threatened by the question I mentioned earlier, "Who's the first person you ever felt really loved you?" you might try some questions I heard recommended by John Sandford. What was your father like? Did he give you affection? Could you run and jump into his arms? Sit on his lap? Did he play with you? How did he discipline you? [Unfortunate if he didn't.] Was warmth and love connected with it? Was he fair? What kind of occupation did he have? Was he gone a lot? Was he home most evenings? If you worked around the house, did he notice? Did he affirm you? Was he critical? How did he relate to your mother? Did they give affection? Respect? Did they argue in front of you? Fight? Did he drink a lot? Was he violent?

You may ask a person to fill in the blank in this statement: "My father made me feel like _____." You could do the same with your mother and others. One young person went through a whole list this way: "My mother gave me a picture of myself as unwanted, because of all her problems. My father made me feel like I wasn't even there, nonexistent. My maternal grandmother made me feel stupid, inadequate, a failure, criticized, defensive, manipulated, unable to please. My maternal grandfather made me feel special. My paternal grandmother made me feel important. My paternal grandfather I never knew. My brother made me feel competitive. My peers and teachers made me feel dumb and worthless. My foster father makes me feel secure. My foster mother makes me feel the mercy and forgiveness of God, so I can forgive and love myself."

Answering these questions may help you pinpoint some areas to pray about. What parents and others near us think of us is like a mirror reflection to us of ourselves.

Developing a Healthy Father Image

A man who is a friend of ours says, "I had a very weak father image, because my dad was gone most of the time, and didn't seem to show much interest in me when he was home. I loved him, and I knew he loved me, but I really didn't want to be like him. I had very little sense of what 'father' means.

"I never could get much satisfaction thinking about God as my Father. Jesus I could appreciate, but God the Father was rather a blank to me. After many years as a Christian, I received a new release of the Holy Spirit, and my faith began to open up to me in a special way. I came to realize what it meant to have a Father in heaven. God truly was my *Father,* in every good sense of the word. I realized that a father is someone who is always on your side, no matter what. He loves you, so he's going to insist that you 'fly right.' He'll discipline you, if you misbehave, but he is always *for* you.[33] The concept of fatherhood, which my earthly father had failed to impart to me, suddenly became clear by the revelation of the Holy Spirit." In Psalms 68:5 God says to the fatherless and those with damaged fathers, I will be "a father of the father-less."

Dr. Robert Frost says:

> I remember a young teenage girl, crying for joy after the Holy Spirit had revealed her Heavenly Father to her through the love of Jesus. A hurt in her life regarding her earthly father had been healed, and she was released from a bondage of years' standing. She confessed through tears that it was the first time in her life she knew what the love of a father was really like! To find Jesus is to find the Father; to know Jesus is to know the Father; to love Jesus is to love the Father; for Jesus said, "I and my Father are one" (John 10:30 KJV).[34]

In soul-healing prayer, our love for Jesus increases, and as it does, it increases also for the Father and the Holy Spirit. We cannot be touched by one without the other.

The person who needs to understand what "father" means, can look at good human father figures for help, too. Joseph, the earthly foster father God chose for Jesus, must have been an exceptional father. Dr. Frost describes him this way:

> As a young child, Jesus received the first impressions of what His Heavenly Father was like from the life, words and face of Joseph. How often He had felt the strong, reassuring arms of Joseph around him during childhood times of sadness and disappointment. It was Joseph's tender touch which comforted the little boy whose finger was cut in the carpenter shop. It was to him He went for fatherly counsel and wisdom when perplexing affairs bewildered a young lad who was learning the ways of this world.

> Joseph, I am sure, was always careful to relate the boy, Jesus, to His Heavenly Father as He matured, and godly responsibility and dependence were divinely developed. Upon the death

of Joseph, the transfer from the earthly relationship to the heavenly was complete. Joseph had fulfilled his God-given responsibility well.[35]

Sometimes the foster father of Jesus Christ isn't given the importance due him either. Maybe you'd like to take time to thank God for Joseph.

Interpretations of Visualizing Jesus

Time and again in soul-healing prayer I have seen the power of visualizing or sensing Jesus. He is the healer, and so His presence is most important. He knows where it's best to lead a person into a scene, and where not to. It's necessary to follow His guidance.

How Jesus appears to someone during prayer often reveals a picture of how that person sees his or her earthly father. In Maxine's vision, she had Jesus' and her earthly father's roles mixed. It was important for her to realize that they weren't the same. She wasn't seeing Jesus as He is: unconditional love. Yet it was good that the problem came out, so she could understand it. If a person doesn't want Jesus to touch him in a prayer scene, it's obvious he has a problem with his earthly father or father substitute. If Jesus is in the scene but at a distance, it may show that the person is feeling estranged from his father.

When a person can't see or sense Jesus at all, it may show he or she hasn't forgiven father or mother from the level of the will; or perhaps it's just too hard a scene to get into at the moment.

Some people are so damaged that they can't see nor sense Jesus' presence at all. The best thing to do then is to go to the memory of the time when they first accepted Jesus; or when they were aware of God working in their lives at another time, and relive that happy scene with Jesus. Then move on gently from there.

"No Blame Can Be Attached"

In the book *House at Pooh Corner,* one day Piglet and Pooh are visiting Owl in his tree house, when a wind storm occurs knocking the house over, turning everything topsy-turvy. Owl is looking for someone to blame, and decides Pooh must have done it, since he is sometimes a clumsy, fat little bear. Piglet, the little pig, stands up for his friend and explains it was the wind.

> "If it was the wind," said Owl, considering the matter, "then it wasn't Pooh's fault. No blame can be attached to him." With these kind words he flew up to look at his new ceiling. . . .
>
> "Piglet!" called Pooh in a loud whisper.
>
> Piglet leant down to him.
>
> "Yes, Pooh?"
>
> "What did he say was attached to me?"
>
> "He said he didn't blame you."
>
> "Oh! I thought he meant—oh, I see."[36]

If you were around our house from time to time, you would hear Dennis and me quoting these words: "No blame can be attached." After all no one wants to be blamed! Not even us.

Ever since Genesis, people have looked for someone to blame. In soul-healing prayer, we're not doing this. We're asking God to show us the source of problems, so we can pray for relationships to be healed. Our attitude should never be one of finger pointing.

Blame is not the name of the game. Parents aren't to blame nor are we. Hurts just naturally occur in a fallen world. We can blame ourselves *only* if we are unwilling to take necessary steps to resolve our difficulties.

Some people blame parents because they don't know who else to blame. But it isn't important whose fault it is; it is important that healing is available. God turns everything to good—if we let Him.

Children often feel neglected by a parent simply because of circumstances. A handicapped or sickly younger child can take time and attention from the other children, so these youngsters may grow up not feeling as loved as they should. One woman lost both parents, mother at birth, father at two. Her whole childhood seemed gray and unhappy until she prayed about her parents' deaths, and was healed. God was then able to remind her of many happy scenes in her youth which had been repressed. She said, "The gray of my childhood has turned to technicolor."

Fathers and mothers have important roles to fill. Without God's help, parenting is a well-nigh impossible task. With God, it can be a satisfying adventure.

For almost as God, your children love you. And you can lead them, and show them the way to God.

10

Adults Hurt, Too

IMAGINE YOURSELF

Imagine yourself on the road to Emmaus,
Imagine yourself on the road standing there.
When all of a sudden a man walks beside you,
A man who seems quiet and hasn't a care.
A man who's familiar, but somehow not known,
Who opens your eyes then leaves you alone
        Standing there on the road.

Imagine yourself on the road to Damascus,
Imagine yourself on the road standing there.
When all of a sudden a bright light surrounds you,
A bright light that blinds you and look you don't dare.
When out of the light rings a voice crystal clear,
That causes your spirit to leap when it hears,
        Standing there on the road.

Imagine yourself on the road by Jerusalem,
Imagine yourself on the road standing there.
When all of a sudden the sky parts before you
A man rises up and He walks in the air,
And soars to the heavenly gates whence He came
And you're left alone to carry His Name
        Standing there on the road.
        Standing there on the road.

"Imagine Yourself," one of a number of songs written by my step-
son, Conrad J. Bennett. Copyright © 1976.

"The Spirit of the Lord God is upon me; because the Lord has anointed me to proclaim good news to those in need; He has sent me to heal the brokenhearted, to set at liberty those who have been bruised; to preach deliverance to the captives, and the opening of prison to them that are bound; to preach recovery of sight to the blind, and the Lord's year of liberty;

"To console them that mourn in Zion; to give to them beauty for ashes; the oil of joy for mourning; the garment of praise for the spirit of heaviness: that they might be called trees of goodness, the planting of the Lord, that He might be glorified."

When Jesus read from Isaiah 61 in His home synagogue at Nazareth, He applied it to Himself, letting us know what He came to do. In the foregoing paragraphs, I have made a composite of Isaiah 61:1–3 and what Jesus read, as recorded in Luke 4:16–20.

Have you been bruised and torn? Has your heart been broken? It's hard to bring good news to others when life has dealt harshly with you. Satan knows this, and he, directly or indirectly, has caused and instigated the hurts, to keep you from being effective.

Adult hurts don't involve as many repressed memories as childhood ones, so it's easier to find the needs. On the other hand, the fresher memory of things done to us recently may be harder for us to pray about in simplicity. It may be harder to forgive recent offenses.

Some Hurts of the Adult

What are some of the adult problems that need to be prayed about? The *World Almanac* for 1981 says that for every two marriages in the United States there's one divorce. No matter for what reason, a marriage has been dissolved; if you initiate a divorce, you will likely have guilt to cope with. Conversely, if a marriage of many years breaks up because your mate wants a divorce, you may feel deeply rejected. When someone's been part of you ("one flesh" the Scripture calls it), and leaves, it's as if some of your physical heart had been removed. You may feel lost and empty. Bitterness and hate can creep in.

Divorce leaves scars, not only to the couple but to children involved. The answer is not sympathy and well-meant advice, but to pray for healing for your soul about specific scenes where the hurts occurred.

Jesus said He came to heal the brokenhearted, to anoint the bruised soul with His healing oil. A lovely woman prayed about the scene in which her husband asked for a divorce. She said with joy, "Oh, Jesus' words to me are like warm oil!" Then she, through Jesus, spoke forgiveness to the woman who had married her former husband, and she felt deep release and healing.

Other occurrences which may hurt you as an adult: a broken engagement; being involved in an accident, especially if you caused it; seeing an accident, especially if someone near to you was in it, or caused it; hospitalization; surgery, especially if disfiguring; chronic illness; rejection by children or mate's children; loss of job or career; problems with neighbors; persecution for one's faith; close friendship broken; disappointment in someone you admired; battle over inheritance; menopause (both male and female!); retirement; loneliness; neglect when elderly; death of someone loved.

Others are: an alcoholic mate; an unfaithful mate; drug abuse; psychological wounds from war or imprisonment, or being held hostage; giving up a child for adoption; having an abortion; being exposed to abusive language; or physical cruelty.

The psalmist said God would "lead us beside still waters, and restore our souls" (*see* Psalms 23:2, 3). Can He do this in such circumstances as those just listed? Of course. I'll tell you some I know of.

The Death of Someone Dear

One of the greatest hurts is the death of a mate. My husband Dennis's first wife died in 1963. They'd been married for many years. In 1969, while he was working on his book *Nine O'clock in the Morning,* we spent a week or two at the Springs of Living Water Retreat in Chico, California. In a little cabin in the woods, he wrote the chapter about Elberta's death, but found it so difficult he was in tears. He said, "I'm going for a walk, honey. I can't touch that chapter again." While he was gone, I sat down, read the chapter, and cried, too. Then I realized someone was going to have to help him with the finishing touches and so worked on it myself. He regained his composure and was able to come back and work with me.[37]

I believe writing that chapter was healing for him, though even since then, from time to time we've needed to pray further about the memory of Elberta's death. The wound was deep, but Jesus' power is sufficient to meet the deepest needs.

When someone very close to us dies, questions prey on our minds: *Why didn't we do things differently? Why didn't we do more?* The questions don't help; they either torment us or condemn us, or both. There's nothing that can be done now anyway. It's especially hard if we weren't there to say good-bye.

Soul-healing prayer can "do something about it." Not only does it help us with life right now, but it can prepare us to face that last journey ourselves when the time comes.

Tom's Last Journey

Let me tell you about Tom. He was a personable young man, nineteen years old, the son of Bob and Bette Anderson (good friends of ours). He had two lovely sisters, Robin and Stacey, all deeply believing Christians. Everything was going well for him, until one cold winter night in January 1979, he was knocked off a fishing boat while at sea and drowned.

I attended the funeral. The minister apealed to each person present to be sure that he or she was in right relationship with God, as Tom was, and there was a call to commitment at the end of the service. Twenty or so young people responded, and Tom's parents, and his sisters, prayed with each one! What an example of God turning evil to good, and giving grace and strength in time of need!

Spiritually, and in God's love, the family was able to handle the terrible shock with courage. But there were still soul hurts to work through. It was over a year later that Tom's sister Robin phoned to say she needed help dealing with the memory of her brother's death. A prayer partner (whose name also happens to be Robin), Robin Blanchett, and I met with her. As we talked with this attractive young woman, we didn't feel we should begin by praying about her brother. We met three times and prayed about other memories, each of which were healed, before it seemed the right time to pray about Tom's death.

When that time came, we were in my study. My prayer partner asked, "Robin, are there any hurtful memories before Tom's death you'd like to talk about?"

Robin nodded. "Tom was like my very best friend, we always had a close relationship. I guess that's why I'm only now getting around to coping with his death. But you know how it is with family. Even though you love them dearly, there are those little things that annoy you at times. Tom seemed to be jealous of my new boyfriend; after all, *he'd* always been first in my life, so we had a few words about that! Then he had been taking me to work, and I hadn't been helping him enough with gas money. So—more words."

I suggested, "Robin, let's ask Jesus where He wants us to begin praying."

The three of us joined hands. "Where do you see Jesus coming into the scene?" I asked.

"Oh," she responded, "Jesus is there where Tom and I are arguing over the fact that I accidentally put a tape into his brand-new tape deck—*backwards!* Jesus looks sad because we're so wrapped up in material things.

"Now I see myself getting ready to go to work, and I am walking by the couch where my brother was sleeping the last time I saw him. (I decided not to wake him up, so I never got to say 'good-bye.') I see Jesus kneeling there beside Tom, and I'm going in to join Him while my brother sleeps. I'm just sitting beside Tom, running my fingers through his soft, blond hair, and loving him. I feel so peaceful inside. Everything seems okay now."

We could see the relief spread across her face. Everything *was* okay.

Angela Westmoreland of Brentwood Bay, B.C. writes:

"On Friday morning, March 20, 1981, you were speaking at a meeting in Victoria and referred to Isaiah 61:3, which talks of God exchanging 'beauty for ashes, the oil of joy for mourning.' You asked those who were mourning or grieving over the loss of a loved one to see Jesus in the room with that person the last time we saw him. I couldn't believe how incredible it was that you should know (which, of course, you didn't, but the Holy Spirit did) my greatest sorrow was I was not certain my husband was with Jesus, in spite of the fact the Lord had kept him alive in a miraculous manner, until he accepted Jesus as his Lord and Savior.

"After his passing, the enemy had had a field day taunting me, and I was never able to fully release my husband. On that Friday morning, I was able to see the scene of my husband's death. I saw Jesus in the hospital room lifting my husband off the hospital bed into His arms, as he took his last breath. It was so real and so very comforting that all the deep sorrow which I have experienced these past three years was truly turned into 'beauty and joy.'

"As if to confirm the Lord's blessing, the very next Sunday in church, one of the hymns sung was, 'What a Friend We Have in Jesus,' a hymn I chose for my husband's funeral. Before the healing I would completely dissolve at hearing it, but this Sunday I was able to truly rejoice in the Lord during the singing of it. I know my husband is with the Lord, and I need not weep any more."

For some people time heals quickly, and in a year the grief is pretty much resolved. But some mourn for years, and others for a lifetime. I heard of a woman who after the loss of her son wore black for the rest of her life. People like this need soul-healing prayer.

Release From Depression

A man who suffered from depression told us, "To me it's as painful as having a physical disease." I would go further and say that depression is in some ways worse than physical illness. Someone in intense pain may be cheerful and optimistic, but the depressed person finds no joy in anything, even though he or she is in good health, and has no objective reason to be unhappy.

Depression may be physically caused by hypoglycemia, hormone imbalance, or nutritional deficiencies. It can have a spiritual cause. People who have been involved in cults or the occult can be depressed because they have opened themselves to false spirits.

If we don't know of any such causes, we can assume the depression is coming from hurts in the soul. A person may be deeply depressed because of events in the past that he or she does not remember until the Holy Spirit brings them up, or it may be from something quite obvious: the loss of a job or the death of a friend.

Jesus' question "When did it begin?" (Mark 9:21) is a good way to start, whether the cause for depression is known or unknown. Again, the Holy Spirit will "bring all things to our remembrance" (*see* John 14:26), as we follow His leading.

Remember how Cleopas and his friend were walking back to their home in Emmaus on the very morning of the Resurrection? (*See* Luke 24:13–35.) These two disciples were depressed. They'd left all—jobs, families, friends—to follow Jesus, believing Him to be the Messiah and expecting Him to set up His Kingdom right away. Now their world had collapsed, and they were themselves fugitives. What will happen to them when they get back to their village and their families?

The Man they loved so dearly—the One they were sure was the Messiah—had died like a common criminal on the "gallows" of their day.

When they met Jesus, they didn't recognize Him. How did Jesus handle the situation? He didn't come bouncing up with "Well, it's a beautiful morning! There's nothing to be so unhappy about! After all you're young and you've got your health!"

No, He quietly fell in step with them. And though they didn't recognize Him, He walked along with them, identifying with them in a friendly and loving fashion. He took time to sense their mood. Jesus knows depressed people need to talk out their feelings, so He asked why they were sad. (The Greek word here means "gloomy, sullen.") He knew the answers, of course, but they needed to express themselves.

Paul says to "rejoice with those who rejoice, and weep with those who weep" (Romans 12:15 NKJB-NT). Remember how, at the tomb of Lazarus, Jesus shared in the sadness, even though He knew He was going to bring His friend back to life? (John 11:35).

After the disciples had their say, Jesus began to remind them of all the things the Scripture said about the Messiah, including the fact that He would be mistreated and killed before He established His Kingdom. Their spirits began to be stirred: "Did not our heart burn within us . . . ?" (Luke 24:32 NKJB-NT).

Finally, at supper, *He was known to them in the breaking of bread* (vs. 30, 31), and then disappeared. Did they scurry back to Jerusalem that same evening to tell the others? They sure did! When Jesus reveals Himself there is no more depression!

As with Peter, Jesus' dealings with these disciples is a good picture of how He can deal with us. Through the people praying with us, Jesus asks, "Do you know why you are depressed? When did you first notice this condition? What were the circumstances at the time your depression began?" We tell Jesus exactly how we feel. With Him, we don't have to pretend we don't have problems. Then we listen to His voice and receive understanding and healing. Our hearts, too, are warmed as He speaks to us, either directly, or through Scripture. As Jesus walks and talks with us, depression goes and joy returns.

If you're dealing with a severely depressed person who is unable to cooperate with you or to visualize Jesus, you may need to use the "healing of the memories" kind of prayer. Agnes Sanford, that great lady who has helped so many understand healing, both physical and psychological, originated this type of praying back in the 1950s. (Many leaders in the healing movement today owe their start to Agnes Sanford's inspiration and teaching.) In healing of memories, you don't ask the person to participate. You just ask Jesus to go back into the person's past memories and heal them, trusting God's gifts to guide in the prayer. It's usually helpful to lay your hands on the person's head while you do this. This way of praying can be very effective.[38]

The Lord's Supper

Don't overlook the healing power of Holy Communion (Lord's Supper, Eucharist, Mass, Divine Liturgy, whatever your church calls it). The Lord made Himself known to the disciples at Emmaus in "the breaking of bread." He can do the same to you. Holy Communion is healing for body and soul. As you receive the Sacrament or Ordinance of the Lord's Supper, you can bring your hurting child-self or your adult hurts to Jesus and receive His touch. You can bring your broken heart and your broken dreams to Him, and let His healing love travel down the corridors of your mind and the avenue of your heart's emotions, putting you back together again.

Father Ted Dobson, a Roman Catholic priest with a strong inner healing ministry, taught about the Lord's Supper while in Seattle this year. He said, in effect, bread and wine are universal elements. Bread is a symbol of words and deeds (yours and others), and wine is a symbol of feelings and emotions (yours and others). As the bread and wine are offered, he suggests you offer words and deeds that have hurt you with the bread, and damaged emotions and feelings with the wine. As the bread and wine are consecrated to God, the miracle happens, and when you partake of communion, you receive these things back, transformed by God's grace. You receive the grace of Jesus to live in victory.

God Heals Teenagers

Are teenagers children? Alexander the Great had conquered the world by the time he was sixteen; some of the pioneers who crossed this country in covered wagons were fifteen-year-olds; the apostle John was probably in his late teens when he became a disciple of Jesus; the Jewish boy is considered to be an adult at the age of twelve; even in the modern USA most adult privileges come now at eighteen. Yet our modern teenagers are still treated a great deal as if they were children, so their problems are a mixture of adult and childhood. It's a difficult in-between time.

At a Full Gospel Business Men's Convention in Portland, Oregon, Dennis and I were asked to talk to the young people. I shared with them a little bit about soul healing, and they were very interested, so we prayed with some of them for healing of their hurts.

Some typical problems were:

Being asked by parents to break up with a girl or boyfriend of another faith.

Being "told on" by a sister or brother—the facts misrepresented, and the mother believing the other party.

Getting involved with a cult, and the trauma involved in breaking away from it.

Being treated unfairly. This is one of the hurts that bothers young people most.

A singing group from a Seattle church had been supplying the music. They were very interested in what we had been talking about, and as I began to pray for the young people, four married couples from the group joined me. They had never seen this way of praying, and some of them were weeping as one young person after another was visibly healed and able to release his or her feelings.

Dennis and I left the meeting at 11:00 P.M., but those couples told us the next day, "We stayed on and prayed soul-healing prayer for one another until one A.M.! The Lord did many deep healings, and we realize a piece of the puzzle of how to live effectively as Christians has fallen into place for us. Now we want to learn as much as we can about it so we can help others."

One of the men said, "What fascinated me was that these kids were praying about hurts that had happened an hour, a week, or maybe six months ago, while we adults were praying about things that went back fifteen or twenty years. Yet we were healed just as easily and effectively as they were!"

One of the wives, Ann Marie, was healed that night from a severe trauma in her life.[39] She wrote me the details:

"I was eighteen years old and newly divorced from my husband who had left me and my infant son. After our marriage was over, I was a very emotionally confused and disturbed person. During this time, however, I met a sweet and sensitive young man who wanted to take care of me and my son. He had a job waiting for him in Europe, and wanted us to go with him.

"One night we went to a dance and fought on the way home. I said unkind and stupid things I didn't really mean. When we got to my house, it was about 3:00 A.M., and we were still upset. He left me that night with the remark, 'If you still want to go with me to Europe, I want you to call me in the morning.' I didn't wake up that next morning until about 11:30 A.M., and when I did, I rushed out to a pay phone to try to call him and say I was sorry. There was no answer.

"I felt something was wrong. I got a friend to drive me to his house, and when I got there, I went right in because the door was unlocked. I ran and looked through all the rooms, and he wasn't there. I went into the kitchen, which was all glassed in, so you could see the backyard. . . . There he was. He had hung himself.

"My whole world collapsed. The person who had driven me over heard me screaming, came in, and called the police. They were there in a short time. I kept asking if he was alive, and they wouldn't answer me. Finally they said the coroner wanted to talk to me.

"I went to his best friend's house and said, 'You've got to help me,' and he said, 'I hate you! You killed him.' I left and went to my sister's, and she said it was my fault too. I finally ended up at a friend's house, and she put me to bed.

"The funeral was on my son's first birthday, and his [the boyfriend's] family all held me responsible because of a letter he had left addressed to me (which I didn't receive until some years later). This situation and the guilt being laid on me from so many, kept me bound for nine years. I was unable to forgive myself, and unable to forgive anyone else.

"As my friends gathered around me to pray, at the Full Gospel Convention, I could not see Jesus at all; I was absolutely convinced my boyfriend's death was my fault. After a lot of prayer, I could see myself in the car fighting with him. I saw Jesus sitting in the backseat, and He showed me that in the car was where I needed to begin forgiving. With Jesus' help, I asked forgiveness, and I forgave myself. Then Jesus spoke to my heart and said, 'Your responsibility for what happened ended when you got out of the car.' What a release!

"The next place Jesus appeared was in the house after I found my boyfriend. The Lord just took me and held me on His lap and comforted me. I wept many tears of release. My friends and I prayed a lot that night, and I asked the Lord to tell my boyfriend that I was sorry, and then I forgave the people who blamed me.[40]

"Before my healing I had prayed for deliverance of attitudes of unforgiveness, criticism, and judging others, but I never experienced release of the compulsion to act this way until my friends helped me pray that night for emotional healing. The Lord showed me that these wrong attitudes had been in some way hooked up to this tragic experience in my life.

"I knew I was healed, but I wondered how I would handle my son's birthday that year, since every year prior to this, I relived that horrible memory. That year, on my son's birthday, I received a letter from the city's largest daily newspaper, saying they wanted to buy an article and pictures I had done on my church for the Sunday edition! It was like a gift from Jesus. Every year now, I have a new memory to replace the bad one. Since this time of praying for healing, the Lord has even continued to create more wholeness in this area and others. I thank God also for two beautiful children, and a wonderful Christian husband."

One fine young man asked for prayer at one of our seminars in Hawaii. Though he was a spirit-filled Christian, he had a compulsive habit of stealing. He stole small amounts of change, here and there from his friends. He knew it was wrong but couldn't seem to help himself.

I found that as a child he had been falsely accused of stealing and beaten severely with a strap. As he relived the scene, Jesus stepped in and took the beating for the young man. He began to weep, and as he realized Jesus' love for him, he was healed and able to forgive his father.

Another young man had been falsely accused of selling drugs, and was for a time ostracized by his church and family. He had then left home and really gotten into drugs, thus fulfilling the erroneous rumor. In healing prayer, Jesus spoke to him deep within and said: "I know what it means to be falsely accused. I was called a drunkard, a blasphemer, an impostor. I know how it feels."

The very heart of soul-healing prayer is that Jesus took our sins (and the sins of others against us) upon Himself when He died and rose again in victory. He shares that victory with us.

What About Older Folk?

An older person may need help with a whole lifetime of hurtful memories, and may be coping, too, with new hurts from the problems of aging. Feeling "put on the shelf" can be difficult. Older persons may feel they are burdens to their families, whether they are or not. They often battle loneliness. They miss their friends who have gone on ahead of them. All these things can respond to the healing love of Jesus.

Remember, when dealing with older folk, that it is only the body that ages. The believer's spirit has no age, and the soul may still be caught back in the Hurt Child. In fact it has been observed that senile people sometimes regress to the time in childhood when a hurt occurred, which hasn't been healed.

My father, known to many lovingly as "Dad Reed" was strong and vigorous well into his eighties. He lived in his own house and took care of himself until the last few months of his life. He was a strong Christian. A year or so before his death, I had the joy of praying for him for some of his hurts. I found him very open. He had already received much healing, when he was released in the Holy Spirit in 1954.

We prayed first about a recent accident which had made him afraid to drive again. It hadn't been his fault at all. A young fellow had bashed in the side of his car while it was parked in the supermarket parking lot. Dad was upset about it though, and afraid it would invalidate his insurance, because of his age, if he filed a claim. We prayed about it; Dad forgave the young man, and let Jesus heal the fears. (Our family got the car fixed for him.)

I then suggested we pray about a fight he'd had with one of his brothers. Dad, then a senior in high school, was asked to leave home because of this fight. He didn't talk about it very much, but I knew this must be one of his most hurtful memories. It must have been a serious blow to his self-confidence. Though an intelligent and warm person, Dad never seemed to feel quite as good or as important as other people.

As we prayed, he could see Jesus in the living room with his father, brother, and himself. He knew he was wrong to have slapped his brother, but seeing through Jesus' eyes, he realized his father's reaction was far more severe than the situation warranted. Through Jesus, Dad asked his father's and brother's forgiveness. Then he forgave his father, and Jesus reconciled the three of them. Dad could then see Jesus going with him while he got on the train to make his way in the world at age seventeen.

He had never been to a big city before. God truly had been with him as he'd gone into the railroad office, knocked on the door of the head agent, who asked him if he was a Christian, interviewed him, and promptly gave him a job! That was about 1910, and Dad said "jobs couldn't even be bought." In spite of this door opening to him so soon, he must have experienced deep rejection and loneliness. Reliving it with Jesus helped to heal those memories.

When my Dad died at eighty-five (almost made it to eighty-six!), I knew he had no qualms about seeing his father and brother Scott again. The last time I saw my father was just before he died. Although in a semicoma and unable to speak, he gathered all his waning energy to lift his hands saying without words, "Praise the Lord!"

How about you? What kind of healing do you still need? What great plans did you have which fell apart? What hopes and dreams have toppled? What has burned to the ground? Gather these ashes in your hands, lift them up, and offer them to God. He promised to give you beauty for ashes. Give Him your broken dreams. Give Him broken relationships. You'll see. He'll make something beautiful out of them and out of your life.

Prayer: From Ashes to Beauty

Dear Father God,

I offer these ashes of my life up to You. It doesn't seem a very lovely gift to offer, but You instructed me to do it.

I give You ashes; please give me beauty;
I give You my grief and mourning; please give me joy;
I give You heaviness of soul and body; please give me garments of praise.

I give You my heart. Please mend its brokenness. Lost pieces, replace with Your healing love. Take away any bitterness; fill me with Your sweetness. Thank You for pouring into my emptiness the warmth of Your presence. Thank You for these gifts, Lord.

In and through my life, Lord, be glorified. Thank You.

In Jesus name, *amen.*

11

Getting to the Roots

BIRTHDAY OF A CHILD OF GOD

Oh, birds of the air, break forth into joyful song . . .
Oh, little trees of the field, clap your hands . . .
Oh, majestic mountains, echo the laughter of the wind . . .
Oh, friendly waves of the sea, dance with joy . . .
Oh, silent rocks, shout the news . . .
It is the birthday of a child of God,
And all creation is glad thereof.

All of creation is bubbling with excitement.
The flowers appear on the earth today in glorious apparel,
And the birds break forth into joyful song.
Even the angelic hosts are rejoicing with anthems of praise.
For this is a special day of gladness and celebration . . .
It is the birthday of a child of God!

MILLIE KOCHENDORFER

If you want to get rid of a dandelion in your front lawn, you shouldn't just chop off the top of the plant (the leaves and the flowers)—that's only a temporary solution to the problem. You need to get at the root, and a dandelion root goes very deep.

It's not much different with problems in the soul. You may hack away at obvious symptoms, but the healing will not be complete until you get at the roots. How is that to be done?

The roots of some problems may just go back to a time in adult life or teens, but most of the really deep roots go back into early years. Some go all the way back to birth, and others even further to prenatal days—even back to the time of conception itself. These are the most difficult ones to discover and deal with.

In soul healing, we are not digging to find the roots. Digging around in the subconscious can be risky business. But the Holy Spirit can bring things to the surface, where we can deal with them through prayer.

Dave's Taproot

Dave was one who needed to find the roots of his troubles. In 1978, Dennis and I were at a church in the Midwest. Dave and his wife, Laura, asked if I would pray with them.[41] He said he had been actively homosexual from age eleven until he received Jesus and was released in the Holy Spirit in 1969. At that time, he had given up the homosexual life-style, and been prayed for for deliverance. This happened before he and Laura were married in 1972.

He said that ever since he had closed the door on his old life, he had had psoriasis, skin eruptions which troubled him greatly. Did this mean, he wondered, that he still had repressed emotional hurts from his background, which were manifesting themselves?

"That's possible," I said, "why don't we pray about it?" So he, Laura, and I went downstairs and found a room where we could be uninterrupted.

"Let's go back to beginnings," I said. "What hurts do you remember in your early life that might have caused your problem?"

Dave told how, at the age of eleven, he had been sexually attacked by several boys in a vacant house. Obviously we needed to deal with that memory. I asked Dave, "Can you see Jesus anywhere in the scene?"

"Yes," he answered, "but I feel so unclean I don't think I can go to Him."

"But Dave," I replied, "Jesus loves you unconditionally. He doesn't love you any less because of what happened to you."

Dave visualized his eleven-year-old child-self going to Jesus. As he saw Jesus receive him with love, tears began to roll down his face. He was able to tell the boys who had abused him that he forgave them and set them free—and himself, too. He asked God to forgive him for any willing participation on his part.

But we weren't back to the deepest roots of Dave's troubles. As we continued praying together, he said, "You know, I'm seeing something I used to have a recurring nightmare about when I was little. It's a kind of swirling pattern, like a sandstorm, picking up things around it. When I used to dream about it, it would keep increasing in size, and I'd wake up screaming. I'm seeing that pattern now. What do you suppose it means?"

The swirling pattern made me think of the way an unborn child might see things, so I said to Dave, "Do you think this may involve something that happened before you were born?"

As he considered this, all of a sudden he began to sob. "Oh!" he said. "My father's trying to kill me! He's beating on my mother's stomach!" He explained to me later that his father was an alcoholic with a violent temper, especially when drunk, and that he had been furious when he found his wife was pregnant.

As Dave released his pent-up feelings, his wife, Laura, and I felt led to rock him gently, like a baby. I repeated over and over, "God's presence covered you in your mother's womb. [*See* Psalms 139:13.] Jesus is there with you, Dave. He will protect you. Everything's going to be all right." After three or four minutes his deep sobbing subsided.

Then we prayed about Dave's birth itself. As we did, he cried out, "I don't want to be born! I want to die!" (This death wish could have been picked up from his mother, as well as his father. She was afraid to have the child because of her husband's anger.)

"But, Dave, Jesus wants you to live. He created you. Be willing to be born for Him."

Dave could remember the bright lights in the delivery room. I said, "Psalms 22:9 says, 'God delivered you from your mother's womb.' Jesus is there with the doctor, and everything is going to be fine. Whether anyone else wanted you then or not, Jesus did. He is delighted you are being born because He knows you're going to become a child of God. Feel His arms holding you. He's proud of you. You're just what He wanted!" As he saw Jesus with him, receiving him, rejoicing over him, Dave's weeping ceased completely, and he relaxed.

Because the birth was a cesarean section, he was kept in an incubator for several days. We claimed Jesus' love for Dave to heal any feeling of rejection due to being separated from his mother. He could see the nurse tending him, giving him the mothering he needed.

Then Dave, through Jesus, told his father he forgave him for not wanting him, for trying to kill him before he was born. Dave had no memory of his mother or anyone else ever telling him that his father had done this. Evidently it had been buried in Dave's subconscious from before his birth, and God the Holy Spirit had brought it to mind as we prayed. God is the best Psychiatrist imaginable!

There was still more to pray about, but that prenatal memory seemed to be the deepest root, the taproot of his troubles. Dave recalled something that had happened when he was nine that caused some disillusionment about his mother, so we prayed about that, and Jesus took care of it. We then prayed specifically for his psoriasis to be healed. All this had taken about an hour and a half. God had already done a deep and lasting work, but as we parted, I encouraged Dave and his wife to continue praying further for soul healing, and to try to find someone to pray with them.

Recently, after quite a bit of effort, our secretary, Sue Williams, located Dave by telephone. I talked to him, and asked if he would be willing for his story to be shared in this book. He willingly consented.

"It's been three years since we prayed together," I said. "Bring me up to date. How's everything going?"

Dave replied, "You know, Rita, I've felt a cleansing and growing from that day on. I was able to release my mother. All through my childhood and youth, I'd try to protect her from my father when he was drunk and violent. I'd gotten into a kind of bondage about it. Even though my father was no longer threatening her that way, I still felt the responsibility. I suddenly realized I didn't have to protect my mother any more, and somehow I've been freer to relate more fully to my wife as a result."

"Oh, that's so great, Dave!" I said. Once again I felt a great happiness in my heart, as I realized how willing Jesus is to heal us, and how simple it is to guide people to receive His healing.

"You know," he went on, "being able to release my mother prepared me for her death a year later. It would have been terribly hard for me otherwise. Of course I was sad to see her go, but all I could say at her deathbed was, 'Praise the Lord! Praise the Lord!' "

"That's beautiful!"

"I used to have a fear of even seeing my father, but that's gone. I'm free from my father's domination. When, through prayer, I had let go of anger towards my father, and forgiven him, from that time on he was more able to accept me. He's changed, too. You know, he faithfully took care of my mother during the last few years of her life, while she was sick; and before my mother died, there was a full reconciliation between them—with forgiveness on both their parts.

"Rita, I've had a great deal of healing from homosexual thought patterns, and I feel a growing release from them. Do you think my feelings toward men could have been because I was looking for my father's love?"

"I believe that's true," I replied. "You were programmed to feel rejection from your father before birth. Growing up, you experienced the same thing. The old enemy loves to work through people to set up these destructive patterns as early as he can. With you it was very early. That recurring dream in your childhood was trying to give you the message from your subconscious, but you didn't understand it." (Deeply rooted problems like this are difficult to deal with. The negatively programmed subconscious can work exactly opposite to what the reason or conscious mind knows is right. Dr. James A. Stringham, a Christian psychiatrist says: "The subconscious mind is not subject to reason.")[42]

Dave said his skin condition was much improved and wasn't a bother to him anymore. He felt he was receiving a gradual healing. Although they hadn't found anyone to join them, he said he and Laura had continued to pray together. I sent my love to Laura, and hung up the receiver, rejoicing. I thanked God, too, for a wife who would stand with her husband, the more injured of the two, in his recovery.

Just as I was completing this book, I again talked to Dave on the phone. He said, "Rita, this year we had the best Father's Day ever!"

Life of the Unborn Child

Studies are revealing more and more about the life of the unborn child. Scores of books will tell you that the child in the womb is sensitive to its mother's moods, negative as well as positive. The child may share the mother's hormonal reaction to stress, and experience the same hurts she did. If there are already too many children in the family, the feeling of rejection could be carried to the fetus. Too often a woman is instructed about everything else, other than how she thinks and feels during pregnancy.

The child in the womb is not subhuman. The *fetus*[43] is a human being, and even though the soul and body may be in early development, the spirit is there—and aware. The tiny brain is already recording impressions that come in through the newly forming senses. Investigation reveals that you didn't hear only gurgling body noises and the drumbeat of your mother's heart when you were in the womb, but that you could hear her voice, and the voices of those around, too. The mother's voice sets its permanent impression on the child. Luke says that John the Baptist was filled with the Holy Ghost from the time he was in his mother's womb (Luke 1:15), and that when Elizabeth, in her sixth month of pregnancy, was greeted by her cousin Mary, who was carrying the unborn

Jesus Christ, ". . . the baby leaped in her womb" and she was filled with the Holy Spirit (1:41).

John the Baptist apparently could hear at six months, even though an unborn child's hearing isn't supposed to be fully developed until the beginning of the seventh month. "It has been medically proven that fetuses, as early as the third month of gestation, can react to sound. Professor Ogawa of the Tohoku University, a pioneer in this study, with the use of an electro-encephalogram, got an over fifty percent response in four to five month old fetuses."[44]

It's no surprise that the newborn shows a strong preference to his mother's voice from the start. It follows that mother's words and sound of her voice are highly important, as well as what the child *in utero* hears and records from the rest of its environment.

If you're a mother reading this book, don't be worried because you didn't always radiate sweetness and light to your unborn child! God turns everything to good if we let Him, and it's never too late to pray for your children, no matter how old they are. Some of these ideas should be helpful, however, to future mothers and their children.

My older brother, Dr. Bill Reed, physician and surgeon, has for years encouraged expectant fathers to lay hands on the wife's abdomen and pray God's blessing and love on the unborn child. What a great beginning! If mother and father walk wisely in God's love, the unborn child has an ideal environment during those months of first growth.

In those days you "had it made"! You were cozily surrounded by a bump-proof water bed, thermostatically heated. You were fed, wastes removed, and received oxygen—all with no effort on your part. Everything was done for you with no waiting. You spent much of the time sleeping peacefully, but you were also active. You probably started sucking your thumb at two months, and you started kicking your feet at that time too (although your mother doesn't feel it until about the fourth month). Lots of fun!

Perhaps memories of this carefree internal life are why many people like to sleep on water beds! Are we trying to relive those earliest days? Dr. Hajime Murooka believes rocking chairs and hammocks remind us of the enjoyable rocking movements in the womb.

Halfway through the pregnancy, the baby begins to lose some of its freedom. As it grows, the space becomes more restricted, the baby is forced to curl into the fetal position.

The Drama and Trauma of Birth

"Birth is a tidal wave of sensation, surpassing anything we can imagine," says French obstetrician Frederick Leboyer in *Birth Without Violence*.[45] Not many of us were born following the wisdom of the Leboyer method. The lights are kept dim in the warm delivery room; the newborn infant is placed directly on its mother's tummy, as it adjusts to its new world. The umbilicus is not cut until it ceases to pulsate a short time after birth. This is so the youngster is not suddenly forced to begin breathing by a spank on its bottom to make it cry in fear and anger, but allowed to make a gradual transition from umbilical feeding to breathing oxygen. The child is then put into water at body temperature to ease the change from floating weightlessly in amniotic fluid, to the new immobility and gravitational pull of the earth. The child is taken out of the water and then put back in, like a game, helping in the first minutes of adjustment.

For most of us, the introduction to planet earth was truly frightening: bright lights, loud noises, chill air, separation, aloneness, roughness. This could especially be true if your mother was hours and hours in labor; if you were born breech;

or if your birth had to be assisted by instruments. Anxiety and fear in later days may have begun in the birth canal. Claustrophobia is only one of the possible syndromes which could result.

Apparently all of us have experienced the fear that comes with birth, although for some it was more difficult than for others. Leboyer also says, "Nothing is forgotten—birth least of all."[46] He says further, in effect, contractions are to the child both a pleasurable hugging sensation, and a frightening crushing sensation. The child decides to be born (unless labor was induced) and moves in that direction. This stimulus sets labor in motion. The child is pushed into a tunnel. Fear is without limit. Then fear changes to anger. The infant fights trying to free itself—fights for life. Death seems almost certain. The first cry is automatic because the thorax constricted by external pressure is suddenly relaxed and opens wide. This first breath also burns greatly; stunned by the pain, the baby pauses, then breaths easily. At birth there is freedom, but a feeling of nothingness. The child wants to go back to its mother. The child has fought for life, and has won. The child thinks, "I'm here alive, but Mother is gone. What have I done to her?" It is important the infant be immediately reassured that Mother is safe.

What can be done about this trauma of birth? Jesus can heal it. He had a lot to say about being born. He said to Nicodemus, "That which is born of the flesh is flesh, and that which is born of the Spirit is spirit" (John 3:6). He said, "Unless a man is born of water [physical birth] and the Spirit [the new birth], he cannot enter the kingdom of God" (3:5 NKJB-NT). In fact, without this new birth he can't even see the kingdom (3:3).

The second birth, the "spiritual" birth, begins the process of healing the hurts of physical birth. Some deep inner hurts and fears are immediately healed when Jesus is accepted, and the new life in the Spirit begins. (There are many hurts we have been healed from, perhaps even going back to our birth, which we won't know about until we see Jesus face-to-face.) Further healing occurs when the person receives the release or Baptism in the Spirit. Beyond that, most will benefit by soul-healing prayer as we are describing here.

Life After Birth

I've prayed with numerous people who couldn't love or feel loved by their mothers. If the child felt rejected at birth, it probably rejected its mother; then the mother rejected the child, and a vicious cycle began which may continue on into adult life. Once a person recognizes problems which stem from being separated from his or her mother at birth, healing can begin.

Nancy was born with a birthmark on her face.[47] When her mother first saw her, she screamed. Already feeling rejected, the baby was taken into surgery right away to have the birthmark moved as far as possible into her hairline. Imagine the emotional impact on this newborn child!

Infants may be separated from their mothers for various reasons:

If your mother and you had a long and hard delivery;

If you were born by cesarean section;

If there was an Rh blood factor problem, so that your blood had to be completely exchanged after birth;

If you were premature, and had to be in an incubator for a time;

If, for some reason, you had to have special attention or surgery immediately after you were born; or

If your mother was incapacitated for several days or weeks after your birth.

The most drastic: if your mother died at your birth, or

If you were born out of wedlock and put up for adoption.

Much is being discovered and written about "bonding" between mother and child. There is a sensitive period shortly after birth, in which a special attachment between infant and mother develops.

Unless the mother has received a lot of sedation during labor, the baby will be alert. The mother should caress her infant, look it in the eyes with full eye contact, talk to it, and then feed it. This skin-to-skin contact in the first thirty minutes gives a deep closeness or bonding. It's good for the father to be there, too, if at all possible, so the child can be bonded to both parents.

Many doctors have growing concern about harmful effects of separating newborn babies from their mothers. The traditional silver nitrate eye medication is delayed, and a radiant panel is placed over the nude infant to keep it warm, while the mother, in privacy, can hold the baby against her bare chest; or the mother and child can be covered with a warm blanket.

The adoptive parents can put the diapered baby on the mother's and father's chests in turn, skin to skin, as they play with it in the morning, for a similar effect.

Fathers and Daughters

Following one of our "Healing of the Whole Person" seminars in California, I received a letter from a young woman by the name of Wendy Kilkenny which illustrates how important it is for a father to have early contact with the baby. Wendy writes:

"My dad was gone from home in my early years due to army duty. This memory has been hurtful for me until the group prayer we had at the Seminar. In the healing vision, on the day I was born I saw my mother place me in Jesus' arms, and then I didn't see but felt and knew that Jesus carried me every place my dad would have. My dad came home on leave; I saw him standing there in his uniform and felt such love and gentleness from Jesus as He walked over to my dad and placed me in his arms.

"As Jesus did this, I changed from the baby into the toddler and that's when the healing took place. That little girl threw her arms around her dad's neck, and there was such a union of love. I have had many inner healings, Rita and Dennis, some big, some small, but this one was very special.

"I realized that all through my childhood I made my dad pay for not being there when I was a baby, and then in later years blamed him because he wasn't the loving dad he should have been. You know the Lord was so gentle, too, in showing me it was my revenge, and not my dad, that was the problem. I feel no condemnation, no guilt, just relief and amazement. Now Dad and I can start being father and daughter.

"My parents came to visit us the other day and I shared what God had done to heal my relationship with my dad. He fought back tears as I told him I was so sorry, and I loved him and wouldn't have any other dad. You can imagine the healing that took place between us! God is so good."

Do You Need Prayer?

One person I know finds it frightening to think about being confined in his mother's body. It gives him claustrophobia, he says. Obviously he needs to pray about it, but if he can't start there, he may need to have later problems dealt with first.

On the other hand, there are those not ready to pray about later hurtful memories who will be more comfortable starting to pray about prenatal days. Let the Holy Spirit lead you.

If you are "works" oriented, and think you have to earn your position with God, it will help you to remember that God was with you long before you could do anything useful, or earn approval. Praying about prenatal times and experiencing God's acceptance from the first has helped such people.

One woman was prayed with for healing of her birth experience first; then she worked her way back, almost week by week, to her conception, which was the most painful memory of all. Seeing Jesus there at the beginning helped her forgive her parents for not being married when she was conceived.

Sometimes it's helpful to ask God to show you your parents before you were born. If you can't accept your parents as they are today, or as you last remember them, perhaps you can accept them as they were earlier on, and allow God to give you love for them.

Male and female choices of identity usually begin early. If your sex wasn't acceptable to one or both parents, you may need to forgive them from this very beginning and accept yourself too.

Ivan Futter, an Anglican priest in British Columbia, said to me, "When you begin praying, take time to be quiet and wait to see if the person can hear God calling his or her name. With some, this may happen."

And it has. I had prayed about conception before, but never waited to see if God might speak to the person directly at this time. Isaiah 49:1 says, "The Lord has called me from the womb; from the body of my mother He has called my name" (*paraphrased*).

One woman said at a seminar, "My parents didn't name me until I was six months old. They just called me 'Baby.' This bothered me, because I interpreted their slowness to mean I was unimportant, and it wasn't worth the effort to name me. As we prayed in the group," she continued, "I heard Jesus deep within call my name. He knew what I was going to be called even before they knew. It made me feel so good and worthwhile. He called me by name from my very conception!"

Another young woman had changed her name to fit an astrological analysis of her personality; her husband, who was very easygoing, went along with it. After she had been renewed in the Holy Spirit, she tried to decide which name she should keep. I advised her, "God knew your name from the beginning. Why don't you ask Him what He calls you?" She did, and when she heard Jesus call her by her original name, the doubts were settled, and any final dregs of astrology expelled.

Please note that praying for prenatal times has nothing to do with hypnotism or hypnotic regression, any more than other soul-healing prayer does. The child in the womb has memories, and the Holy Spirit is recalling those memories, just as He can and does in later life. We are asking the person to recognize that Jesus was with him or her from the first moment of conception. The person's will is submitted to Jesus, not to another person.

There may be other hurts you want to pray about, other than those listed already: you were unwanted; adopted (adopted children, although much wanted, often have need of healing due to being rejected by their biological parents—or feeling rejected); parents' first reaction to child was negative; at birth or shortly after, you were turned over to relatives or others for a period of time, and then taken back by your mother. If your mother or father died during the first few years of your life; if you had an alcoholic parent or parents; if your parents separated while you were young—all these are hurts you may want to pray about.

Are there any root causes that need healing in your life? Did reading some of these chapters bring some to mind? There is absolutely nothing that Jesus can't heal, if you let Him. He wants to more than you know.

A Scriptural Order for Praying From Conception to Birth

As I searched the Bible, I was delighted to find so many Scriptures on prenatal times and birth. God obviously wants us to know what He thinks about it. I've put verses here month by month, to help you meditate on how God made you, and His unending love for you. See Jesus with you from your very beginning—healing, protecting, and loving you.

You don't need to pray all the way through nine months at one time. You can pray in either direction, conception to birth or birth to conception, whichever seems the most helpful.

I. CONCEPTION

Hear Him call your name. You were chosen before the foundation of the world!

Scripture: "The Lord has called me from the womb; from the body of my mother He has called my name" (Isaiah 49:1, *paraphrased*).

". . . He has chosen us in Him before the foundation of the world, and we should be holy and without blame before Him in love" (Ephesians 1:4 NKJB-NT).

". . . the sheep hear his voice, and he calls his own sheep by name . . ." (John 10:3 NKJB-NT).

See Jesus with you when you were conceived. He was happy about you. If there was anything wrong with the circumstances of your conception, see Jesus comforting and forgiving your parents. Speak forgiveness to them through Him. (Add your prayer here.)

Prayer: Lord, You chose me from before the foundation of the world! Long before I was created, I was in Your mind and heart because You know all things, and You knew I would be conceived. You were there at the time of my beginning, and called me by my name from my mother's womb. [*Pause and reflect.*] Even if no one at that time wanted me, You did. You rejoiced because You loved me and knew I would become Your child. My beginning was made holy with Your presence.

II. FIRST MONTH

His presence was with you when your body was first being formed. Within twenty-one days, the beginning of your heartbeat could be detected.[49] Spinal cord and digestive system are in the beginning stages. In your fourth week, your circulatory system is forming like an elaborate tree of life network.

Scripture: "For You possessed my reins [motivational life]: You covered me in my mother's womb"[50] (Psalms 139:13, *paraphrased*).

See your tiny self in the palm of Jesus' hand, which is gently holding you. Know that you're loved and all will be well.

Prayer: Your presence is like a soft comforter, dear Lord. Because You'll be with me now and always, I feel secure.

III. SECOND MONTH

Like a plant ready to sprout, small buds appear, which will become arms and legs. You're over an inch long by the eighth week. Eyelids are half-closed. By the end of this month it was evident which sex you were. God approved of you and your sexual identity from the very beginning.

Scriptures: "Before I formed you in the womb I knew and approved of you ..." (Jeremiah 1:5 AMPLIFIED).

"Thus says the Lord that made you, and formed you from the womb, I will help you; fear not ..." (Isaiah 44:2, *paraphrased*).

See Jesus with you, approving of you. See His satisfaction that you are a boy (or girl), as He planned you would be. Accept it and rejoice in it, too. If your parents wanted a child of the opposite sex, and made you feel in any sense unwanted or inferior, forgive them through Jesus. (Add your prayer.)

Prayer: Thank You, Jesus, that there's nothing I have to do or can do to gain Your approval; You've given it to me. I accept the sex I am. Thank You that there is nothing to fear, as You guide my growth and progress day by day.

IV. THIRD MONTH

Thank God for creating you. Arms, legs, face, and body are taking shape, as though being sculptured from within. Hands and feet are fully formed. Eyelids are fused. The water that surrounds you, giving buoyancy is not stagnant, being replaced many times each day. You are enveloped in a life-sustaining system. Nutrients flow in, wastes are carried away, oxygen is received, all effortlessly.

Scripture: "I will praise You; for I am fearfully and wonderfully made: marvellous are your works ..." (Psalms 139:14, *paraphrased*).

Jesus is continuing to care for you, and watch over you. Your brain is growing and developing and being filled with His love and knowledge of Him.

Prayer: When I think of the miracle of my creation and how well I'm cared for, I want to praise You. You thought of everything for my comfort, growth, and protection. With my heart I praise You, and want to praise You all my days. Thank You, Lord Jesus.

V. FOURTH MONTH

You had been moving your feet since the second month, but even though you weighed only about four ounces, your mother felt your movement for the first time. She knew you were alive! The old-fashioned word for this was *quickened.*

Scripture: ". . . God, who gives life to [quickens] all things . . ." (1 Timothy 6:13 NKJB-NT).

See Jesus, standing by your mother, and smiling happily at her joy, as she feels your life moving in her. He takes her hand and blesses her.

Prayer: Thank You, Lord, that my mother felt my movement this month, and knew all was well. My arms and hands, feet and legs, are fully shaped. She is beginning to know me now; my personality is beginning to show. When rocked, I settle down and rest. Thank You for the gift of life, dear God. Thank You for quickening me.

VI. FIFTH MONTH

Your mother began to "show" that she was pregnant. She may have been embarrassed by this. All your internal organs except lungs are now fully developed.

Scripture: "There is no fear in love; but perfect love casts out fear . . . (1 John 4:18 NKJB-NT).

Jesus is with you as your senses are developing, and you're becoming more aware. He's comforting your mother for any embarrassment or fear she may be feeling. And He's comforting you.

Prayer: Lord, I receive Your love to cast out all fear. Please heal me of any negative effects from my mother's emotional agitations, or from any negative words or actions of anyone else around me. Thank You for my mother and the life and nourishment I have received through her.

VII. SIXTH MONTH

You are covered from head to foot with a protective ointment (called *vernix caseosa*), and spiritually God's anointing presence is covering you, too. A kind of peach fuzz appears over your body, and hair begins to grow on your head. You know your mother's voice and can hear others around you, too.

Scriptures: ". . . as soon as the voice of your greeting sounded in my ears, the babe leaped in my womb for joy," said Elizabeth to Mary in Luke 1:44 (NKJB-NT).

". . . You anoint my head with oil; my cup runs over" (Psalms 23:5, *paraphrased*).

Jesus is anointing you with His oil of joy. He laughs with you as you leap for joy, just as John the Baptist did as an unborn infant, when he sensed the presence of Jesus.

Prayer: Thank You, Jesus for anointing me this month in a special way. Even as John the Baptist jumped for joy at Your presence, so do I! Your anointing is upon my head and covers me, even as the ointment You created to protect me, covers me. Thank You for Your joy that will always stay with me.

VIII. SEVENTH MONTH

All the parts of your body are completed this month. Early this month your hearing is completed, and your eyes open. You listen to your mother's heartbeat; it is well known to you. Later blood changes, so it can carry oxygen, and your lungs are fully developed. Your weight doubled since last month. It would be safe to be born after this time.

If there's anything at all lacking in your physical body (such as congenital problems), it isn't because God planned it that way, but because you are in a world that got separated from God.

Scripture: "My substance was not hidden from You, O God, when I was being formed in secret and intricately created in my mother's womb . . . in Your Book, all the days of my life were recorded" (Psalms 139:15, 16, *paraphrased*).

Jesus is proud that your body is now beautifully complete. You're looking at Him, and listening to Him. His love surrounds you.

Prayer: Thank You, Lord, that though I was hidden from the world, I was not hidden from You. Others couldn't see me but You could, for You are always with me. Your eyes were watching over me to see that my complicated formation took place properly. Thank You that I'm all put together, and ready for the adventure of being born!

IX. EIGHTH MONTH

You and your mother are at this time psychologically one. She is making plans for your arrival. You weigh about three pounds and you're growing fast. It's getting a bit crowded in the womb, so not much movement is possible.

Scriptures: "For thus says the Lord, Behold I will extend peace to her like a river, and the glory of the nations like an overflowing stream; then you shall be nursed, you shall be carried on her hip, and be trotted on her . . . knees. As one whom his mother comforts, so will I comfort you . . ." (Isaiah 66:12, 13 AMPLIFIED).

"As you know not what is the way of the spirit, nor how the bones grow in the womb of her that is with child: even so you know not the words of God who makes all" (Ecclesiastes 11:5, *paraphrased*).

See Jesus with your mother, encouraging her, and refreshing her. You're sleeping a lot, getting ready for new activity to come. You're sucking your thumb, getting ready for the new activity of drinking. Jesus is speaking to you, telling you everything's all right, and that He will be with you to comfort you.

Prayer: Dear Jesus, I thank You for my eighth month, and for

Your continuing presence with me. Thank You that You're holding me safely in Your hands. Thank You that You know the mysteries of childbearing. With You here, all will be well.

X. NINTH MONTH

Normal term of pregnancy is 280 days. You are ready to be born. Jesus is there to deliver you.

Scriptures: Jesus said, "A woman giving birth to a child has pain because her time has come; but when her baby is born she forgets the anguish because of her joy that a child is born into the world" (John 16:21 NIV).

"But You are the one who took me out of the womb.... You are my God from my mother's belly" (Psalms 22:9, 10, *paraphrased*).

". . . it pleased God who, separated me from my mother's womb, and called me by his grace" (Galatians 1:15).

Tell Jesus: "I'm willing to be born and to come into this family. I accept them and ask You to give me a special gift of love for them. I'm willing to go to them, and I know You'll go with me." Jesus is standing with the doctor or midwife to help in your birth.

See Jesus holding your mother's hand, and calming any fears she may have. Something is happening. Waves of pressure sweep over your body. The steady heartbeat you've come to know quickens. It passes. Your buoyancy is altered; more pressure. You're propelled down a course that seems too narrow. Hear Jesus speaking to you while you are still in the birth canal, encouraging you not to be afraid of the dark and the pressure.

Your body begins to tingle during a new wave of pressure. Now the pressure on your head is at its greatest. It stops; your head is free. Then pressure on your shoulders; then freedom. As you see yourself being born, Jesus receives you, and takes you into His arms. He gently cleans off your face and looks into your eyes, and you are bonded to Him in love. Then He gently places you on your mother's tummy, so you can look into her eyes, and be bonded to her. Jesus gently massages your back, and smiles at your mother. You take your first breath comfortably. After the cord has been cut, Jesus picks you up again, and washes you in warm water. When dried, He takes you to your father, who holds you lovingly awhile. He, too, looks into your eyes, and you are bonded to him.

Then Jesus turns to the doctor and nurse or whoever else is present and says, "What a beautiful child! Just what I wanted!"

Prayer: Because I'm accepted and loved by You, Jesus, I'm willing to be born into Your world. Please take the effect of any fear or pain of birth away from me. Heal any claustrophobia from being too long in the birth canal. Heal effects of the harsh bright lights in the delivery room. If the doctor held me by the feet, and spanked me to get me to breathe, heal the memory of that, and from any vertigo from being upside down. Heal me from the pain from my first breath. Heal me from fear of the loud noises when I first came out in the world from the muffled quiet of the womb.

I know that I'm not responsible for my mother's pains in labor, or for any illness she may have suffered due to her pregnancy, or my being born. If anyone blamed me for such things, I forgive them, and release them, and release myself from all blame. (May add your prayer here.) Thank You that You bore both my pain and my mother's pain on the Cross.

(If you were not a full term baby, revise the foregoing accordingly. No matter what kind of a birth it was: normal with head first, breech birth, head wrapped with umbilical cord; cesarean; long labor; instrument birth; Rh blood-factor complication—God's presence can take the fear away. If at your birth, your mother was ill; you were ill; in an incubator; separated from your mother for some time; had surgery, or any other hurts—let Jesus meet the needs.)

XI. FOR THE ADOPTED

If you were put up for adoption right after birth, Jesus wanted you just as much as if you had been born a prince or princess in a palace. No baby is unwanted or rejected by Him.

Scriptures: "Can a woman forget her sucking child, that she should not have compassion on the son of her womb? Yes, they may forget, yet I will not forget you. Look, I have engraved you on the palms of My hands; the walls of your life are continually before Me" (Isaiah 49:15, 16, *paraphrased*).

"Although my father and my mother have forsaken me, yet the Lord will take me up [adopt me as His child]" (Psalms 27:10 AMPLIFIED).

God is "A father of the fatherless . . ." (Psalms 68:5).

Make the same visualization as above of Jesus receiving you from your mother's womb. See yourself bonded to Him as He picks you up in His arms. If there is no one for Him to show you off to, see Him lifting you up and showing you off to His Father in heaven!

Through Jesus speak forgiveness to your natural father and mother. Release them, and release yourself.

Prayer: Lord, I thank You that even though my father and mother did not, or were not able to, receive me, You received me in Your love and bonded me to You. Thank You for those who did take me in [adoptive parents, foster parents, others]. Thank You for Your care for me all through my life since then.

Even the best parents don't always have unconditional love, but Your love will bridge any gap that may come. Thank You that You can even create a father's and mother's love for me if I need that.

You may want to take some time now, after reading these Scriptures and prayers, to close this book and pray your own prayer. Let God bring to mind spontaneously the verses, parts of verses, and thoughts which are especially for you. Remember He loves you unconditionally!

(*Later you may want to make up your own list of personalized scriptures month by month, with God's affirmations to you.*)

12

A New Start for Susie

Let me tell you about Susie Johnson, a young lady brought to Shade and me in mid-January 1980 by her mother, Carol. Susie had been born in England, and the family moved to the USA when she was two and a half.

I'll quote from a letter I received from her mother:

"Susie seemed to be a happy, carefree child, and we saw no problem until she was in sixth grade. She was the easiest of our three daughters to deal with, always ready to accommodate, and we seldom had any problems with her.

In sixth grade, Susie developed a horrendous cough. We took her to doctor after doctor, and no one could find anything physically wrong. She spent some time in the hospital, while specialists scratched their heads over her, but they could never find the source of her problem. The cough left of its own accord, and life went on.

"Susie continued with her coughing episodes intermittently, and every six months or so, she had to be taken out of circulation for three or more weeks. In 1978 we returned to England for seven months. The cough continued. Later that year we moved to Everett [Washington, USA], and she entered seventh grade. From then on we were in trouble. She coughed her way through the year, and by the summer, she was a nervous wreck.

Susie Stops Eating

"On July 27, 1979, Susie decided she was too fat, and stopped eating. It was as simple as that! She lost more than forty pounds in weight, and still would not eat. We went to every doctor in creation, from stomach specialists (her reason for not eating was that her stomach hurt) to psychiatrists, and nobody seemed able to help."

When Susie first started not eating, Carol said, the cough had subsided, but when she threatened to force Susie to eat, the cough came back and remained. If Susie was coaxed into eating, she would throw the food up again. Having encountered this particular syndrome before, I knew how serious it was, and how it baffled medical doctors and psychologists. It's called *anorexia nervosa,* a pathological loss of appetite.

Carol continues:

"Finally, I came to my senses. I realized no doctor was going to be able to help us, and I got on my knees and asked God to help. I had always believed in Him, but by no means had any sort of personal relationship with Him. I did not really think He would intervene in our everyday lives. How wrong could I be?

"With the help of Christian friends, I learned how to really pray, and the comfort I received, and the strength I gained saw both Susie and me through some very dark moments. My husband, Peter, was gone so much at that time due to his work—we only saw him on weekends, if at all. He felt terribly lost trying to cope with the situation when he did come home."

When Carol brought Susie to us, she told us things were at a very low ebb. Susie was showing no signs of improvement, and her mother felt there was a wide distance between them, with very little point of contact. "I was beginning to be really afraid that she was going to fade away before my eyes," said Carol.

The First Visit

When Susie and Carol came to our house, they seemed a typical mother and daughter. Susie was fourteen years old, but she looked much younger. This wasn't too surprising, since at the time of our first meeting, she hadn't eaten solid food for nearly six months. She was existing, her mother told us, on chocolate milk and tea, and, of course, her body was not growing as it should.

Some may ask at this point, "What's wrong with living on milk?" Milk alone cannot sustain health in adults, much less in growing teenagers. There's a mystique about milk being a perfect food, but as a matter of fact, milk is only a complete food for babies, preferably human mother's milk. There is no iodine or copper, even in fortified whole milk; there is only a trace of iron; it is very low in vitamins B and C. There is no bulk.

From ages ten to fourteen girls need fifty grams of protein a day. Milk does provide a complete protein, but in order to get that fifty grams, Susie would have had to drink approximately six eight-ounce glasses of whole milk daily. Normally she drank three, her mother said. Then, too, she was drinking chocolate milk, and chocolate hinders calcium assimilation. Also, the milk Susie was drinking was pasteurized, which meant that the enzyme phosphatase, which enables the body to use the calcium and phosporus in the milk, had been destroyed, along with most of the vitamin C. The wonder is that the child could have survived her extended fast as well as she did.

We found Susie to be a nice-looking young lady, rather reserved upon first meeting. I thought it quite brave of her to meet with two adult women she didn't know. Every few minutes she coughed harshly, and I knew this must be very annoying to her. At the outset, it was Susie's mother who answered most of our questions, since Susie wasn't very talkative. We didn't ask much about her history but tried to make it more like a friendly visit.

Susie said she didn't like her mother to be fat. We found that while Susie had lost forty pounds, her mother had gained fifty-five, perhaps reflecting her anxiety over her daughter's condition. (Actually Carol didn't strike me as "fat." She's plump—a nice-looking woman.) Susie told us she has two younger sisters, the older of which is only thirteen months younger than Susie. Susie said about her, "Vicki grew even in this last week; or maybe I shrank."

We found out that, like most young girls, Susie likes horses. But, she told us, she fell off one in California and has been frightened to get on horseback since. This seemed a nonthreatening situation to pray about for a beginning, so Shade and I explained to Susie how we wanted her to let Jesus come into the scene that had caused her to be afraid of horses. We joined hands around the kitchen table.

Susie recalled the experience and said, "Yes, I see Jesus while I'm riding on the horse. When I fell off the horse, He put me back on, and now He's walking along beside me." She smiled. "Jesus looks happy." We then prayed and ordered any destructive powers affecting her life to leave, and asked the Holy Spirit to fill in empty areas.

We prayed about the uneasiness she must have felt at the age of two, when she left her grandparents and moved to another country. (Carol said about that move, "Susie had to cope with a mother who spent her whole time crying!")

The next day I called Carol, and asked how she felt about our time together. She said she was pleased, since Susie had recently been noncommittal when asked questions. On the way home, Susie commented, "That wasn't so bad!"

Prenatal Prayer Helps

Four days later we met again with Susie and her mother. Shade and I decided to begin by praying for Susie's prenatal days, from the time of her conception, until her body was fully developed and ready for birth.

We prayed about any fears Susie might have picked up during these months because her mother had a heart condition. We did this using the "healing of memories" way of prayer, just telling Susie to relax, while we prayed for Jesus to heal these areas, not asking her to participate actively.

Next time we met, Susie said she had had a good week. "My little sister, Sarah, had laryngitis." What this meant, apparently, was that little sister couldn't draw much attention to herself (since she had to keep quiet), so Susie got more of the limelight!

We prayed with Susie about her birth. She participated readily, and said she saw Jesus in a white robe holding her, and herself all pink, as a newborn baby would be.

Leaving Carol and Shade to talk together, I invited Susie to join me in my study. "Susie," I asked, "what do you like to talk about?"

"Horses first of all," she responded, "then dogs. I have a dog and I want a horse but I know it would probably be too expensive."

"Well, Susie, you could rent a horse. That wouldn't be too expensive. Not very many people can afford to own their own horse." Carol told me later that near their house there are stables they've driven by for a year, but Susie had never expressed any interest in the horses. It looked as though our first healing prayer had taken effect!

I asked, "Is there anything special you would like to do?"

"I'd like to go out with my dad for dinner."

Don't Miss the Miracle!

The impact of what Susie said didn't hit me, until I repeated it to Carol later. Dinner with her dad! Susie, who had not eaten solid food for over six months, had of her own free will expressed the desire to eat! That's the way it is with miracles. They can be so "naturally supernatural" you don't notice them when they're happening. Evidently the prenatal and birth prayers had already begun the work of letting Jesus heal Susie.

When Susie was three weeks old, Carol told us, they had moved from England to Wales. Carol had then had to return to London for three months to finish some cases in her legal work. During the same period, Susie's father, Peter, was supervising the building of a house for his family, about forty miles away. Thus she was separated from both parents for that time, while her grandparents took care of her.

We prayed through the first six months after Susie's birth, with special attention on the three months when Susie's mother had to be gone. We emphasized that Jesus was with her all the time, and encouraged her to see Jesus holding her, feeding her, and giving her lots of attention. We helped her to realize that being the first child, she was very special to her parents.

"You, as a teenager, aren't holding it against your mother that she had to be away from you for three months when you were only a tiny baby," I explained. "But that six-weeks-old little girl didn't understand where her mother disappeared to. The baby Susie loved her grandparents, but even they couldn't take the place of her mother. Maybe the little Susie inside still feels rejected, and needs to forgive her mother." That made sense.

Forgiveness and Freedom

Carol looked at Susie, and asked, "Susie will you forgive me for being away from you in those first months of your life?" Susie responded, "Yes, Mummie, you know I do." Both were visibly moved, especially Carol.[51]

Later, Shade and I encouraged Carol not to feel guilty about leaving Susie in the care of her grandparents while she was so young. It's only in recent years that the need for infants to be with parents, and especially the mother, in the first months is being recognized. "Be careful you don't treat Susie any differently than her sisters in matters of discipline," Shade advised Carol. "Her condition and your guilt might cause you to do that."

Hope Howard was at our house on this day. She's very good with young people, so I asked her if she would do an art project with Susie, while we talked more with her mother. Hope said, "Sure! We'll do something I just learned in a course I've been taking." So the two of them took cardboard boxes and made collages of pictures from magazines, gluing them both to the inside and the outside of the boxes. "On the outside you put pictures of what other people think about you, and on the inside how you see yourself," explained Hope. Susie entered into the project very happily.

Carol said she suspected Susie may have started eating on the sly. "When she feeds her dog," she said, "she insists that we all leave the kitchen. I think she's probably getting something to eat, too, but doesn't want us to know!"

Susie Breaks Her Fast

Just a few days later, on the telephone Carol told me, "This week Susie definitely broke her fast. An older gentleman, a neighbor of ours, took her and her sisters out, and bought them pizza!"

The miracle had happened!

Dennis and I were at the airport in Denver shortly after this, and fell into conversation with another traveler, a medical doctor. I told him something of our experiences with physical healing, and he seemed quite open and interested. Then I told him of Susie's healing. "To me," he said, "that is more remarkable than any of the other things you've been telling me about."

Carol told me in a phone call, "I can see the Holy Spirit at work in Susie, and can't get over the change. She is so open with me now, and is eating in front of me. I can't thank you and Shade enough."

I replied, "It's Jesus!"

"Yes, but you're His vessels."

"Okay," I returned, "I'll accept that."

The Healing Continues

Carol sent me a letter recently. She wrote:

I'm sure you saw more changes in Susie than I did between our visits with you. I was so obsessed with the thought that she had to eat, I didn't really notice that her cough had disappeared completely, that she was going to school daily, and keeping up with the work. We were slowly beginning to communicate. We could come to both of you and talk about things that had happened through the week. God was starting the sometimes-painful process of healing.

Susie's eating habits didn't settle down completely to normal right away. The family went to England on a visit in the summer. While there, a very dear friend of Carol's died. Susie sensed how upset her mother was, and they spent a lot of time together, talking about many things they had never been able to approach before. Her mother related, "Susie took the role of supporter, and really grew with it. Within a week of my friend's death, she was at the table every meal, and we haven't looked back since."

Carol's letter continued:

This year Susie has had different trials to face. She entered high school in the fall, knowing no one in her class, and we were afraid problems would develop, but she handled it beautifully. She had no friends at first, but that didn't last for long!

Her health has not been too good, constant colds, asthma attacks, and she had mononucleosis. Her body was truly run down after all the abuse it took last year. However, it has been a great relief to her to go to the doctor and have her ailment diagnosed as something other people have.

Susie is growing in self-assurance every day. Her last quarter was particularly good. The *A*s and *B*s have started coming, and with each one, her confidence has gone up a notch. She understands herself more, and is using strength instead of weakness to get through any situation that develops.

All I can say is, "Thank You, God!"

Lovingly,
CAROL

13

How to Pray for Your Children and Your Family

I see where my children got the problems they have, but what can I do to help them?

If you have open communication lines to them, you can pray the same way for soul healing as you would for yourself or others. If your child is reticent at first to pray about problems in the past, teach him or her first to pray about things that have just happened. If he comes home from school complaining that some bigger kid has pushed him around, help him to see Jesus in that scene, so God can heal it and your child can learn to forgive.

Remember, children visualize easily, so don't hesitate to ask them to see Jesus in the scene they're praying about. Their openness will surprise you.

After you've successfully prayed together several times like this, you can say, "Is there anything else you want to pray about? Maybe something that happened a longer time ago?"

If there doesn't seem to be any opening to pray with your children directly, you can pray for them, even when they are asleep, or falling asleep.

With two- and three-year-olds, who don't have the verbal capacity to express their feelings, you can use finger paints, dolls, or other play techniques to help them work through their problems. Jesus can come into finger-painting scenes very easily!

Dreams

Most children from time to time have bad dreams. Much is simply the subconscious giving back what's been put into it. Perhaps they have been allowed to watch too much television violence and horror. Yet long before TV was invented children were having nightmares. Maybe they'd been reading good old *Grimm's Fairy Tales,* or the *Arabian Nights!* No, TV didn't originate horror and violence for kids. But if youngsters have frequent nightmares or a recurring nightmare, healing is probably needed.

There are preventive things to be done. Teach your child to practice the presence of Jesus, and to visualize Him there at bedtime, and through the night. Teach him God's omnipresence.

If your child has a bad dream, take time to let him tell you about it. Then have him go back through the dream with Jesus and tell you what he sees Jesus doing, and how the dream is changing (adults can do this, too, by the way). Eventually, the child may see Jesus come into the dream itself, changing it, even before he awakens. This should be especially effective with recurring dreams.

Dr. Leboyer feels that nightmares may come from birth memories. The newborn's body is covered from head to toe with a slippery white oil. In order to keep a firm grip, the doctor traditionally holds the child upside down by the feet. This may be convenient for the doctor, but the infant experiences an indescribable vertigo. Leboyer writes:

Those who have had nightmares in which they plunge suddenly into a void are familiar with this sensation. It stems directly from this moment during their birth.[52]

If he or she is old enough to understand, explain this to your child, and pray through birth memories.[53] The memory of the dark birth canal may be the source of the very common fear of the dark children have, and their desire for light.

Bad dreams can also be caused by direct demonic activity, if, for example, the parents have been involved in the occult, thus opening the door to satanic influences. In such a case, the parent or parents need to be sure they have renounced the wrong activities, repented, and received God's forgiveness. Then the house should be blessed, and all wrong spirits both in the house and the people living in it should be ordered to depart in the name of Jesus. This, of course, would apply to relatives or others living in the home, too, if they were involved in the occult.

There is evidence that the influence of wrong spirits can continue in a house where they were once invited through spiritualism or other occult practices. Human spirits do not stay on this earth after death and haunt houses, but it seems that other spirits can and do.

Several years ago Dennis was in another part of the country to speak at a college. A woman came to him and said, "My six-year-old is having terrible nightmares every night. He's always been a happy, carefree child. This isn't normal for him."

"When did it start?" Dennis asked.

"When we moved into the house we're living in now, about a month ago."

To make the story brief, Dennis went to the house and blessed it and the people, including the youngster who had been having the dreams. No more recurring nightmares! We still hear from these folks from time to time.

Blessing of homes goes back very far in Christian tradition. The Orthodox priest is supposed to bless every home in his

parish at least once a year. In fact, it is probably from this custom the idea comes that the pastor should call at the homes of
his people at least yearly. At any rate, bless your house. Go
over it room by room, commanding all evil influences or wrong
spirits to be gone in the name of Jesus, praying under the protection of Jesus' blood. If you belong to a church that has a
custom of blessing houses, have yours blessed by your priest or
minister.

Sticks and Stones

STICKS AND STONES MAY BREAK MY BONES, BUT WORDS WILL
NEVER HARM ME. So runs the old adage. Sounds good, but it
isn't true. Words are powerful things. It makes a lot of difference what you call someone, and harsh words and name calling can do a great deal of harm. Look at the effect name calling
had on Meg in chapter 1. A child may be called unkind names
by other children, or by his parents, which color his picture of
himself for life.

One young man we were praying with said, "My father had
a very bad temper, and he called me a 'jerk' and a 'jackass.' It's
hard for me to forget it."

My prayer partner said, "Why don't we bind those unkind
words" (as in Matthew 18:18). He prayed, "In Jesus' name I
bind the names 'jerk' and 'jackass,' and I command any wrong
influence from them to depart." Then we gently laid our hands
on him and prayed for the Holy Spirit to fill him and replace
the unkind names with the ones Jesus had for him.

After a few moments, he smiled and said, "I hear the words
'prince' and 'precious,' and I see myself dressed in royal robes,
like a prince would wear."

God did something similar for Jim in chapter 2 of this book;

and remember the hurtful words written to Meg, SHE'S NUTS, were replaced by Jesus' words, SHE'S MINE?

Were you, or your children, ever called "dummy," "stupid," "good-for-nothing"? God says you have the power to bind those destructive names and remove their power. Both you and your children can pray this way, then see Jesus in the scene, and let Him heal. Receive the new names Jesus will give to replace the old ones. You will, of course, want to forgive the offender.

Breaking Harmful Generation Ties

Exodus 20:5 says that the Lord visits the sins of the fathers on the children to the third and fourth generation of those that hate Him. This doesn't mean God *wants* to punish people, generation after generation, but that He cannot help it, if they do not stop hating and rejecting Him. There is no way for Him to help them, so the law must take its course, until or unless the pattern is broken.

That breaking begins when someone accepts Jesus, and is born again of the Spirit, but even then, a wrong pattern can continue in the soul. The father with an unhealed soul can damage his son or daughter's soul, and they in turn their children's, until Jesus is allowed to heal. Then the chain is broken.

Sometimes you'll see a pattern like this going back several generations. It may be a fear or prejudice passed along. It may be an attitude. There can be patterns of mental illness or perverse behavior, or even something like spiritualism or occultism.

I was chatting one day with a close friend, a fine Christian man in his later years. He was reminiscing about his grandmother, who lived at his home when he was a young man. "I used to come home late at night and hear Grandma talking to the spirits," he remarked (casually!).

"You . . . what?" I responded, in some surprise. He repeated what he had said.

"Your grandmother was a spiritualist, then?"

"Oh, I guess so. She sure had some 'friends' in there!"

It had never occurred to him that his grandmother's activities had any bearing on him, but I convinced him that we should pray against any wrong influence coming to him from it.

How do you pray about such things? You pray to break the generation ties. You claim the power of the Cross and of the blood of Jesus to sever any stream of wrong influence moving from one generation to the next.

A man saw emotional problems in his wife's family line going back three generations. His wife had had a very poor relationship with her mother because of them. This man attended a seminar and heard about breaking generation ties. He and some friends prayed about it. They named the great-grandmother and placed the blood of Jesus and the Cross of Jesus between her and the grandmother, breaking any bondage. They did the same between the grandmother and the mother; then between mother and daughter.

When he went home, his wife greeted him, "You won't believe what I just did. I phoned my mother and had the best talk I've had with her in years." I don't know whether the husband then told his wife about his prayer, but something had obviously happened through breaking harmful generation ties.

We tend to reproduce ourselves, both good and bad traits. This is one of the reasons why parents need to seek Jesus' healing, and when they're wrong, to be willing to say those words, "I'm sorry. Please forgive me." This not only frees you and your child, but sets an example for him or her to do the same.

What I call the Tarnished Golden Rule goes like this: YOU WILL DO TO OTHERS WHAT'S BEEN DONE TO YOU. Then I add a P.S.: UNLESS YOU'RE HEALED.

If a father couldn't show a son affection, his son will grow up to do the same to his son. If a daughter was domineered by her mother, she will domineer her family. If a child was beaten, he may grow up to treat his children the same way. But don't forget the P.S.

Helping the Adopted Child

An adopted child needs careful and consistent help. If a child has been conceived out of wedlock, and the father is unwilling to marry the mother, it is often best for the newborn child to be adopted by a family that is eager to have it. No matter how loving that adoptive family may be, however, the child may sense that it was rejected by its own parents from the very time of its conception. Even if the adoption is because of the death of the natural parents, the child will not have been able to understand why its parents left, and may still feel rejection. He or she will certainly need more reassuring than your natural children.

Let me share with you a story about a little adopted Korean girl, by the name of Wha. She had been in an orphanage in Korea from the age of three months to three and a half years, at which time she was adopted by an American family. Her adoptive mother writes:

"All this year Wha's sense of insecurity had been increasing. Whenever I would leave her, even for a short trip to the grocery store, she'd sob bitterly, as if I were never coming back. It hurt to watch her, but I didn't know what to do to comfort her or make her understand that she was secure in our family. I had prayed for her every way I knew, and so far had not found an answer for her.

"In early July, I had a great sense of expectancy that God was going to show me what to do and that I would find the clue in Ruth Stapleton's book *The Gift of Inner Healing*.

"In that book, Mrs. Stapleton wrote several crucial things for me. 'Every child needs a mother.' Wha had none, and for a little child that amounts to rejection (p. 49).

" '. . . these early moments of apparent maternal rejection had compelled her to expect rejection . . . rejection creates feelings of loneliness' (p. 56).

" 'Healing of the memories . . . is one means of instilling positive images deep in the mind . . . these images greatly determine how we respond to each moment of life' (p. 65).

" '. . . Removing old material and replacing it with the new is the total objective of the healing of the memories.' . . .

"As I finished reading these words . . . I was sobbing and sobbing. I knew that God had given me a clue . . . a way to pray for Wha.

"Several days later, Wha and I were walking along on the beach, and I sensed that the time was right to pray for her for healing of the memories, and specifically for Wha's separation from her orphanage 'Oh-mah' and fourteen little friends in her group with whom she had been constantly.

"I held her in my arms as we sat on a huge rock by the ocean and told her that I was going to pray for 'Kim In Wha' (her Korean name) and for when she left the orphanage. (Wha had been referring to herself as 'when I was a Korean girl, In Wha,' and 'now I American girl, Wha'—no connection in this dichotomy.) She became whimpery but told me how much she missed her Oh-mah and friends and added sadly, 'They miss me so much too, Mom.'

"With her vivid imagination, we began to talk to Jesus together. We both pictured 'In Wha' in her orphanage room. (How thankful I was that I had been there.) I asked Jesus to come to the door of her room. Wha took it from there with only tiny questions from me to guide her such as, 'And now tell me what's happening,' and so on.

"Wha began: 'Jesus is at the door and He took His shoes off.' She then went up to Jesus (in our guided meditation prayer) and took His hand, and she asked Him to come in and see her friends. Then Jesus told her Oh-mah and her little friends that He had a super family for In Wha, one that He had all ready for her now. Jesus picked In Wha up and held her. He put His arms around her Oh-mah and held her . . . comforting and reassuring her of His plan for In Wha. Then Jesus picked up each of the other children.

"He picked up Wha and took her to the Il San (Holt) Hospital. And she said, 'Mom, that was where I was sick, and you came and prayed for me, and took me to my new home.'

"I wasn't sure if anything had happened. Later that evening, Wha came into my room singing and singing: 'Jesus loves In Wha, Jesus loves In Wha!' "

This mother had found a new way to pray which was very effective, and from her report she has prayed like this other times for Wha's life. At the end of her letter she reported:

"After praying another time (this was for healing of Wha's baby spirit's being rejected and abandoned at three months), my husband and I went on a three-day trip to Alabama. My son, Terry, and Wha stayed at home with a friend. Wha announced as I told her about our plans, 'Mommy, I know you be back; I be okay, Mommy,' and she was!"

A couple who recently attended one of our conferences on soul healing said: "We've always been hesitant to adopt a child, but now we feel we have direction and guidelines to help a child whose emotions need healing. We're going right out to an adoption agency!"

Melissa and Don Stevenson have been taking infants for foster care. Melissa says, "We pray for these brand-new babies with the biblical laying-on-of-hands, praying to break any bondage from the sins of the parents, and asking God's protection over them. We pray also that their new parents will come to know Jesus through their little child.

"Recently we had a little baby boy, Brian; and when we got him from the hospital, he was very tense and clenched his little fists and his head was misshapen and bruised with forceps marks; he looked beat-up from the birth experience. We prayed for him and loved him a lot. We prayed that he would grow up to serve the Lord. When we gave him to his adoptive family, he was a most relaxed baby; his hands no longer tense, but open and relaxed on his blanket." How wonderful when foster parents can help bring a child healing right from the start!

Where to Begin Helping Your Family

The toughest job is often right at home. It's difficult to work with your own family; they know you so well! Don't be discouraged, or feel condemned if you have difficulty reaching those closest to you. Even the Lord Jesus had a hard time with His own family! They said He was out of his mind! They tried to get Him to come home and settle down. (*See* Mark 3:21, 31.)

A woman said to me: "My family needs healing. My husband has problems, my son and his wife have problems, my daughter and her husband have problems; I guess I'm the only one who doesn't have problems. How can I help them?"

I looked at her, trying not to smile. "If all those family members have problems," I replied, "then *you* have problems, too! I think the best place for you to begin helping your family is by starting with yourself." And this is true for everyone. Learn how to pray for yourself. As your family notices the change in you, they're more likely to want you to help them.

It's good for a husband and wife to pray together. Here are two people totally committed to one another, who can share their burdens openly. If one partner has bigger needs, that one may need most of the prayer help, until he or she is strong enough to pray for the other.

But there are pitfalls. One husband said, "I was doing a good job helping my wife pray through hurts in her life, until she got to the part where her family did some really mean things to her. I got so mad I wanted to punch them in the nose, so we realized we had to find someone more objective to help her. I obviously wasn't ready for a while!" A husband and wife team is great to pray for others, because there's the benefit of the combined male and female outlook. Most importantly though, the gifts of knowledge, wisdom, and discernment make any team effective.

Keep in Touch

As Dennis's sons, Steve and Conrad, became teenagers and were emerging into manhood, he didn't know how to express affection to them. They were too old to kiss, and shaking hands was too formal. After Dennis was released in the Holy Spirit, the Lord was able to show him what to do. Hug them! (That was before the days of the bumper sticker HAVE YOU HUGGED YOUR KID TODAY?!)

By labeling emotion and tenderness as "feminine traits," we have deprived our male population of wholesome physical affection. With the work of the Holy Spirit in men's lives today, we see many men no longer afraid to give one another hearty hugs, and to weep in response to God's blessing, if so moved.

You can't always give your children full attention, but you can give them quality time, at specified intervals. On these occasions, listen to your children with as close attention as you would give someone you don't know well and are trying to impress. Watch your body language. Constant yawning, looking at your watch, tapping your fingers, signal to the child what they have to say is not important. Don't be afraid of eye contact. Don't keep interrupting. Let them talk without feeling rushed. If necessary, repeat what you think they've said to be sure you heard correctly. Be a good listener, don't react emotionally to what they share, or you'll cut off their sharing. Ask questions *after* the child has had a chance to express his or herself.

The classic example in this is Susanna, the mother of John Wesley. She was the twenty-fifth child of her father, and she had nineteen children of her own! She wanted to know what she could do as a wife and mother to help bring Christ to the world.

"I resolved to begin with my own children," she said. "I take such proportion of time as I can best spare to discourse every night with each child by itself. . . . There is no mystery about the matter. I just took Molly alone with me into my own room every Monday night, Hetty every Tuesday night, Nancy every Wednesday night, Jacky every Thursday night, and so on, all through the week; that was all!"

John Wesley himself said, "I cannot remember ever having kept back a doubt from my mother; she was the one heart to whom I went in absolute confidence, from my babyhood until the day of her death."[54]

If you keep the lines open, your children will be willing to talk with you too, when really big things come up which need counsel and prayer. Furthermore, you may have the privilege of leading your child to receive Jesus and the power of the Spirit, as well as praying specifically for hurts life has or may bring. Our young people need high quality help with the many challenges they have today.

Even if you, with your busy life, can't give your children lots of time every day, yet as with Susanna, what you give can be *quality time*. We need to give our children as many happy memories as possible to sustain them through life. By the way, "Have you hugged your kid today?"

14

How to Forgive

Probably no one reading this book needs to be told it's important to forgive. We all know we need to, but don't always know how to do it.

Forgiving is next to the "bottom line" in soul healing, and as you've seen, the theme runs all the way through this book. We've talked a good deal about it, but now let's sum it up in a little more detail.

If you just say to someone, "You must forgive!" they may well reply, "I can't and I won't!" One young lady told friends on the phone before she came over for prayer, "If you think you're going to get me to forgive my father, you're wrong!"

They didn't argue. They knew she needed healing before she would be able to forgive. After praying a number of times for other needs, as she came for prayer one day they asked, "What do you think you'd like to pray about today?"

Her response was, "Today, I'm going to forgive my father!" And that's exactly what she did. She was ready.

This highly intelligent and capable young woman had been depressed for years. She said, "For a long time, when I awoke in the middle of the night, there was what I would describe as something like a radio program on low volume going on in my mind, with a stream of negative thoughts. I could listen in if I chose. It was saying things like, 'This world's really an awful place. You know you'll never amount to anything. You just have one failure after another. There's really no reason to live. Why don't you end it all; that's the only way of escape!' (I guess the only reason I didn't do it, was that as a Christian, I knew it was wrong, and was afraid of the consequences.)"

The night after she had forgiven her father she reported, "I woke up in the night, but instead of a stream of negative thoughts on my inner 'program,' I heard songs of praise to the Lord! I was excited, because I knew what was happening was not just because of my own will or determination; it was God at work deep in my heart!"

Everyone who knows her well is amazed at the remarkable change in her.

This chapter isn't near the end of the book because it's an afterthought, or isn't important. It's near the end because forgiving is one of the harder things to do, and you need to be ready for it. Only a healed soul can forgive from the deep level.

Two Ways of Forgiving

Jesus clearly *commands* us to forgive, just as He commands us to love. He doesn't ask whether we want to or not! There is, then, a kind of forgiving which is a sheer act of the will. You forgive because God has told you to, because if you don't forgive, you will block your fellowship with God. You can't nurse a grudge against another person and at the same time walk in the love of God. "If we walk in the light, as he is in the light, we have fellowship one with another . . ." says John in First John 1:7.

"Forgive us our sins, as we forgive those who sin against us" means we are asking to be forgiven to the same extent we forgive others. And there isn't any limit on it! Peter complained to

Jesus, "Lord, how many times a day do I have to do this? Seven times?" and Jesus replied "No, seventy times seven!" (Matthew 18:21, 22). That doesn't mean we keep a tally, and when they reach 490 times, we can stop forgiving! Even though it seems harder to forgive one person 490 times, rather than 490 persons one time each, yet it is possible with God's ever-ready assistance.

There's no sense trying to deceive God about it, and you may have to pray to be made willing to forgive. "Lord, I don't want to forgive Charles for what he did to me. I'm still angry about it. But I know I've got to forgive him before You can forgive me for what I've done, and before I can enjoy Your company, so please make me willing to forgive him. I don't want to forgive, but I *want* to want to!" You may even have to say, "I *wish* I wanted to want to!" God will honor your honesty, and you'll be amazed at how He helps you.

If you haven't made this basic decision of your will to forgive others, you will be blocked from entering into soul-healing prayer. Forgiveness in your will is like opening a door so there can be forgiveness in the emotions. In fact, when we begin to pray with someone for soul healing, and he draws a total blank, or hits an invisible wall, we go back to this step and ask if he's forgiven the offender with his will. Often he hasn't, so we have him pray a simple prayer: "Dear Father, I choose to forgive [*name person*]. I can't do it in my own strength, but I know You're helping me do it. I claim this, in Jesus' name."

The Second Way of Forgiving

The more deeply and fully we can forgive, the more the Holy Spirit is going to be able to fill us with His joy, peace, power, and love. This second way of forgiving goes beyond mental assent, beyond forgiving from the will. It is forgiving at a deeper level. We become able to forgive this way, as our souls are healed.

You don't have to forgive at this level in order to be a child of God, and an inheritor of the Kingdom. You don't have to forgive in this way in order to have your own sins forgiven. Those things were taken care of when you received Jesus, forgave others with your will, and accepted God's forgiveness for yourself.

But this second way of forgiving is important, if you want to be a truly happy and effective person. It reaches deeper into your emotions and into your subconscious. Some people receive physical healing as a direct result of this kind of forgiving.

A major fruit of soul-healing prayer is that you can completely and permanently forgive. As some friends were praying for a distressed teenage girl in church, the young woman looked up with a flushed, tear-stained face and said, "I've forgiven and forgiven, but the hurt's still inside."

God doesn't want you to have to go around the mountain of forgiving the same person over and over again for the same offense. As with the children of Israel, you'd be a long time getting out of the wilderness at that rate, when you could be enjoying the Promised Land.

If you don't forgive someone who has wronged you for *his* sake, you need to forgive for your *own* sake. You know that, yet how often do you try and fail?

Don't despair! You can go with Jesus to the scene of the injury, and see what He would say and do if He could have His way. This opens the door to truly forgiving. It takes away the hurts inside and heals the memory, so you won't be plagued by it any longer.

I received a telephone call one day from Sandra[55] who said, "I've had it! I've tried everything, and my life is a mess. Group therapy helped a bit; the release of the Spirit helped for a while, but now I don't even want to go to church. Sometimes I feel just like I did before—like ending it all!"

This young lady had been trying very hard over a period of many years to solve some deep problems in her life, and she'd made a lot of headway. Now she seemed to be slipping back. When I'd first begun to work with her, I hadn't known about soul-healing prayer, but now I did, God be praised!

"Sandra," I exclaimed. "Don't hang up! I have something more to tell you." Quickly I explained as much as I could. "Is there something that's happened to you recently you need to pray about?"

She responded, "Yes. One of my good friends told me she never wanted to see me again."

"Where were you when this happened?"

Sandra replied, "In class at school."

"Can you visualize that scene?" I asked.

There was a pause. "Yes," she said.

"Okay. Can you see Jesus there?"

"Why, yes," she said, "I can! I see the three of us. He's coming up to us and putting His arms around me and my friend. It looks like He's reconciling us! Oh," she said with a sigh, "that sure does make me feel better!"

I guided Sandra, through Jesus, to tell her friend she forgave her. As our conversation ended, and we hung up the phones, I wondered what the result would be. She called me two weeks later and said she was still feeling released inside. We prayed about another incident before we concluded our conversation.

A month later I was speaking at a meeting in Sandra's hometown. Sandra was there. I felt the Holy Spirit wanted me to speak on forgiveness. Unbeknownst to me or Sandra, her friend was also there, and after the meeting came up to her and asked to be forgiven.

What had happened "in the Spirit" during that phone call had opened the door for reconciliation to take place a month later. We've seen similar things happen a number of times. When you forgive someone, you release them for God to do miracles in them. Perhaps that's what is meant by "What you loose on earth is loosed in heaven" (*see* Matthew 16:19). Forgiveness is exciting and fun!

The culmination of a soul-healing session comes when you are ready to forgive. You've forgiven from your will but now you're going to do it in a different way, this time from the vantage point of where the original hurt occurred.

When you are ready, visualize yourself at the age you were when the incident happened, just as you did in the healing prayer itself, and speak from that age as much as you can. Speak in the first-person present tense as to the person or persons you need to forgive there in the scene with you.

Speak through Jesus, remembering His omnipresence, and say, "Through Jesus, I speak to you [*name of person*]: I forgive you for [*whatever offense*]; I will no longer hold this against you. I set you free, and I set myself free. Jesus has healed me."

But what if the person I need to forgive has since died? Well, in the first place, you are speaking to them as in the past, while they were still on this earth; but in order to avoid even the possibility of seeming to try to communicate with the departed, you may ask Jesus to give the message of forgiveness to him or her. "Jesus, please tell my mother [or whoever it is] these words, 'Mom, I love you. I forgive you. You did the best you knew how. Jesus is healing me from these hurtful memories! Please forgive me too, if I wronged you in any way. I will not hold this against you any more.' "

Some people visualize Jesus speaking from the Cross, forgiving themselves or the offender. Others like to see Jesus in the scene, and let Him forgive the offender first. That makes it easier for themselves to then forgive. When there are numerous people to forgive at one time, one minister we know of suggests you visualize a room; imagine the people to be forgiven seated in it—and beginning with the greatest offender, go to each one and tell him or her you forgive them.

Most of the time after praying for soul healing (and sometimes during), you just spontaneously want to forgive. Rarely does anything have to be said to help bring it about.

Further Thoughts on Forgiveness

We find it helpful to say to the person we're helping, "Remember, when we encourage you to forgive, we're not by this condoning wrongs the other person did to you. We don't like what he did either, and obviously God doesn't, but that's not the point. You're not putting conditions on your forgiveness." When Sandra forgave her friend, she didn't know what her friend was going to do. She wasn't saying, "I forgive you, if you will make up with me." The friend may have felt she had good reason to reject Sandra. No, the important thing at the moment was that Sandra needed to forgive her friend—regardless—and then, as will often happen, the friend was set free to be reconciled.

Remember, too, when you don't forgive your enemy, you are still being controlled to some extent by that person. If you don't forgive, you may also do to others what was done to you.

David duPlessis, that faithful pioneer of renewal, likes to point out that the best way to protect yourself against anyone who has enmity against you, is to forgive them!

As long as you are holding a grudge against another—even though you may feel it is justified—you are letting him or her hold you in bondage, and giving an opening to hurt you further. When you forgive, you take his or her weapons away, and make it possible for God to protect you. He can't protect you in that situation as long as you are unforgiving.

Forgiving doesn't mean you have to accept another's ethics, manipulations, or morality, or make that person your closest friend. If the other person has not yet "cleaned up his act," you aren't expected to have him in your home, perhaps to be a bad influence on your family.

You can know you've forgiven when you can treat the person just as nicely and kindly as any one else; when you don't try to avoid him on the street or at church. Jesus says, "But I say to you who hear: Love your enemies, do good to those who hate you, bless them that curse you, and pray for them which spitefully use you" (Luke 6:27, 28 NKJB-NT).

When I first started trying to obey Jesus' words, I wondered: *What do I pray for my enemies about? Do I pray for them to have lots more strength and energy to proceed more effectively in their efforts against me?* Then I saw the answer: *I'll pray for God's perfect will for them.* [Only He knows what's best.] *I'll pray for them to be healed, so they will feel secure and happy and won't need to put others down. I'll pray for their families to be blessed and helped in every way. I'll pray "in the Spirit" for them.* (I found there were lots of things to pray for.)

If you haven't tried it yet, do so. One man told me he received healing this way. You can't hate very well when you're trying to love. Genuine forgiveness always manifests itself in love.

Forgiving God

This may sound strange, but some folks need to tell God they're angry with Him and to forgive Him. Your "oughts against anys" (*see* Mark 11:25) may include God, and you're not going to get very far if you have a barrier up against *Him*.

There are examples in Scripture of believers being angry with God. The prophet Jeremiah was upset with God on at least one occasion. He asks God, ". . . Will you be altogether to me as a liar, and as waters that fail?" (Jeremiah 15:18, *paraphrased*). That was strong language to use with God, but God understood. Rebellion or anger against God can be very subtle. A person who really believes in God is not easily going to admit that he or she is angry with Him.

It often happens when we are angry with another human being, we don't admit it but simply hold that person at arm's length. We don't let him or her get close, because we don't trust him or really like him. This can happen with a parent. Some people have never expressed anger toward a domineering parent, and would probably not admit they had it, yet they will have a very poor relationship with that parent. It can be like that with God.

Many have been taught that God is directly responsible for everything that happens. It's no wonder they fear Him, and, if they would admit it, are angry with Him. They know they can't fight Him, so they just keep from getting too involved with Him.

It's a good idea to ask the person you are praying with to describe what he thinks God is like. When he has done so, if his picture of God is not like Jesus, the perfect Image of the Father, point this out, and then pray and ask God to reveal His true nature to him. Read him the Scriptures given in chapter 5 on unconditional love.

A good deal of anger towards God is really aimed at childhood authority figures. We have already shown that you tend to picture God as being like your earthly father. You may find that as a person describes how he sees God, and why he is angry with Him, there will emerge a picture of his or her own father (or mother).

Don't be shocked or put the person down if he expresses anger against God. He needs to admit it, and tell God how he feels. As he does this, he will usually see his own error, and will then ask God (or you can guide him to ask God) to forgive him for his rebellion. One person got right into the "nitty-gritty" by going all the way back to the beginning. She forgave God for loving so much that He gave humanity free will, through which evil and sickness came into the world!

After you or the person you're helping has honestly expressed the anger against God, pray in this way: "God, I've sometimes blamed You for what the enemy has done. I've thought You were against me, but now I see that You are a loving Father, and always want the best for me. Please forgive me, and help me remove any barriers I've put up between us. Thank You for Your love and fellowship. In Jesus' name."

Two Ways of Being Forgiven

While we're taking a closer look at forgiving others, let's look also at our own need to be forgiven. It's true that soul healing isn't so much concerned with the "rocks" we dropped into our own stream of life, as with those thrown in by others; but if we aren't repenting of our own sins, and receiving God's forgiveness, we aren't going to be ready to receive His healing.

We may have tried to accept forgiveness for ourselves and failed. "In soul healing," one man said, "the emphasis is on memories of hurts which others caused us. What about the hurts we've caused others? I've been hurt, and needed healing, but I have also caused other people a lot of pain by my words and actions, and for me these seem to be the memories that hurt the most. They were caused by my selfishness, my insensitivity, and although I am told God has forgiven me, and know some of the people have, the guilt weighs heavily on my conscience. How can I know I am forgiven?"

You may have similar problems. Perhaps you, too, have asked God to forgive you many times, but still don't feel He has. What should you do?

Original Sin

What do we need to be forgiven from? First, from "original sin." *Original* means that it's the source or "origin," from which all the rest of our troubles come. All the problems of the human race come from one factor: being separated from God. This separation began when the first human beings broke fellowship with God, and it continues with us when we don't let Him into our lives.

Jesus came to this world especially to bring us back in touch with God, so the cure for original sin is repentance, which means changing your basic attitude, acknowledging that you can't do it yourself, and that you need God. It means asking Him to forgive you for all the wrong things you've done, especially for rejecting Him, and then receiving Jesus into your life as Lord and Savior.

When you accept Jesus, the Holy Spirit Himself comes to live in you, and you are no longer separated from God in your spirit. When you are praying with someone for soul healing, you will want to find out whether they have taken this all-important first step. As we have seen, you can pray with someone for soul healing, even though they are not sure of God at all (chapter 5), but getting the spirit healed by accepting Jesus is infinitely more important than getting the soul healed.

The Second Way

Original sin leads to what is called "actual" sin. People do bad things to one another because they are out of touch with God, and rebelling against Him. Human history is a terrible record of "man's inhumanity to man," but when Jesus died on the Cross, He took care of all that, and when you accept Him as Savior, all the guilt of past sin is taken away.

As you know, though, unfortunately that doesn't mean we stop doing wrong things. We need to go on being forgiven every day. John says, "If we say that we have no sin, we deceive ourselves, and the truth is not in us. If we confess our sins, he is faithful and just to forgive us our sins, and to cleanse us from all unrighteousness" (1 John 1:8, 9). He is clearly referring here to believers, people who have accepted Jesus.

So the second way of being forgiven is being cleansed from daily sins in body and soul. You need to specifically ask God to forgive your sins each day. "Give us day by day our daily bread. And forgive us our [daily] sins . . ." (Luke 11:3, 4). Keep short accounts with God. Make things right as soon as you realize something is wrong.

If you have done something wrong against another person, go to him and ask him to forgive you. Don't put it off—the longer you wait, the harder it will be. Jesus says, "If you're presenting your offering at the altar, and while there, remember your brother has a legitimate reason to be at odds with you, leave your offering there, and be reconciled with your brother; then return and give your offering to God" (Matthew 5:23, 24, *paraphrased*). Jesus goes on to show that you then need to do whatever is in your power to correct the wrong you have done. If you took something that doesn't belong to you, you must, if at all possible, repay it. Notice, though, your forgiveness doesn't depend on making restitution. God forgives you freely, but if you are truly sorry, you will obviously want to make whatever amends you can.

There are situations where revealing what we have done against someone else may cause further hurt to him or her. For instance, if one person says to another, "I've hated you for years, and I'd like to ask your forgiveness!"

The other person is a little stunned, "Well, of course. But— but why did you hate me? What did I do to you?"

"Oh, never mind. It's all okay now. Don't worry about it."

One person has relieved his conscience, but the other is in worse shape than at the beginning! It would have been better for the offender to have gone directly to the Lord for healing and forgiveness.

Also, there are situations where going to the person may cause hurt and scandal, not only to him or her, but to others. In this case, go to a wise counselor whom you know to be guided by the Holy Spirit—hopefully your own minister or priest— tell him all about it, and let him pray with you about what to do. (Remember, too, you are not supposed to be confessing other people's sins, if they were involved, so keep such names confidential.)

Perhaps you don't know where the offended person is now living, so you can't go to him or her in person. Here you can ask Jesus to take care of it, as you did in soul-healing prayer. Similarly, if the person you offended is dead, you can ask God to relay the message to him or her. You should simply say, "Dear Jesus, please tell Uncle Ned this for me, 'Please forgive me for [whatever the offense]. Jesus has forgiven me, and I ask your forgiveness, too. In Jesus' name.'" Since it's against Scripture to talk to the departed, you talk to Jesus and leave the rest up to Him.

You can have soul-healing prayer for your own forgiveness, just as you do for sins of others against you. You can either relive the actual scene with Jesus, as Sandra did, or use creative prayer. In the creative prayer, you let Jesus show you what He would have liked to happen, and let you experience a new picture in your mind and emotions. Shade calls this getting a "Second Chance." In either kind of prayer, you can let Jesus give you new insights into yourself and others, and why you responded the way you did. This is very important if you are having difficulty forgiving yourself—that common problem. Let Jesus speak forgiveness to you.

Don't overlook the value of what my church (the Episcopal church) would call "sacramental confession." It's been abused in the past; that's why many people are still afraid of it.

Yet many Christians use it without knowing. If you have ever gone to your pastor and confided in him something that was on your conscience, and had him assure you of God's forgiveness, you have already experienced this ministry. Formal sacramental confession has the further advantage, though, of being completely confidential, since the penitent is not even visible.

Traditionally, the minister and the person seeking help do not even see one another (in my church, the person kneels at the altar rail, and the minister sits on the other side with his back to him or her). The penitent person *then tells God* what it is he or she needs to be forgiven for, in the presence of the pastor. The pastor can then assure of God's forgiveness. This kind of confession can be very liberating.

Anything told to a priest or minister in these circumstances is totally confidential. He is supposed to forget it, and never bring it up or refer to it, unless the person gives permission. The sin is forgiven, forgotten, just as though it had never occurred.

Declaring God's forgiveness is part of the ministry of the people of God, just like healing. There are times in the ministry of soul healing when you will find yourself "hearing a confession," and if so, you need also to assure the person of God's forgiveness, in your own words, and in words of Scripture. Anything told you must of course be kept in strict confidence. Again, don't overlook the power of the Holy Communion, the Lord's Supper to minister God's forgiveness (chapter 10).

Forgiveness Is Liberating

Forgiving others, and receiving forgiveness, sets you free to love God and reach His highest potential for your life. It keeps communication lines open to God and prayers being answered. It's good for your health! When you turn your eyes on Jesus, are healed, forgive, and begin to praise the Lord, the enemy doesn't stick around long!

Here's a "check list" of people you might need to forgive: parents, or others in that role; brothers, sisters, husband or wife; children, grandparents, aunts, uncles, cousins, and other relatives, including your in-laws; teachers, neighbors, doctors, officers in the military, policemen and other law-enforcement people; priests and ministers, church officials.

There may be others you can think of, but these may help stir your memory. You may also need to forgive institutions: the army or other military group; church, denomination, government, nations, nationalities—and not forgetting God and yourself.

Janet Biggart says, "We have a lot of wrong ideas about what forgiveness is. I did myself. It was God Himself, while listening to what He was saying in my heart, who helped me forgive someone I needed to.

"This is what He said to me: 'Janet, when you forgive it does not mean you agree with him; it does not mean he was right; it does not mean what he did was right in My sight.'

"You see in my heart I had sort of said, 'God, I cannot forgive this person because what he did was so very wrong. It was wrong in Your Law too. So how do you expect me to forgive this person, when he's not only hurting me but other people?'

"The Lord said to me, 'Janet, the reason you need to forgive him is *because* he's wrong. If he were right, you wouldn't need to forgive him!'

"You see, somewhere in our thinking many of us have come to the conclusion that if we forgive somebody it's because, 'He's come to me and repented and said he was wrong.' It's true we do this, but the kind of forgiveness God wants us to have is *unconditional forgiveness.*"

It is possible to live without holding any unforgiveness in your heart against anyone. That's a worthy goal to aim for. When that isn't the case, you have something to pray about. All the way through life you will be forgiving and being forgiven. It's worth taking some time to understand, and learn how to do it then, isn't it? From the Cross, Jesus forgave you unconditionally, yet you needed to accept Him and His forgiveness to make it yours. Through Him, you, too, will be able to forgive others—*unconditionally.*

15

Deliverance Brings Healing

Deliverance means being set free from the control or influence of wrong spirits.

Some readers when they see the word *deliverance* may think we've left all reason behind, and plunged back into the Middle Ages. Others may judge, "People in the Bible were not really possessed by evil spirits; they were only mentally disturbed, and Jesus healed their neuroses and psychoses. When the Bible says Jesus encountered evil spirits and cast them out, it's just a prescientific way of putting it." I understand what they mean, as there was a time when I would have felt this way myself.

C. S. Lewis in his preface to *The Screwtape Letters* wrote: "There are two equal and opposite errors into which our race can fall about the devils. One is to disbelieve in their existence. The other is to believe, and to feel an excessive and unhealthy interest in them."[56]

As usual, Lewis is "right on." It's difficult to see how anyone who takes the Bible seriously can disbelieve in the existence and activity of Satan. Was it just an imaginary person who challenged Jesus on the Mount of Temptation at the beginning of His ministry? (Luke 4:1–13). Was Jesus just speaking figuratively when He referred to "This woman . . . whom Satan hath bound . . ."? (13:16). Whom was He referring to when three times in the Gospel of John He spoke of "the prince of this world"? (12:31; 14:30; 16:11).

Some Christians, while not doubting Satan's existence, absolutely deny that he, or his cohorts could gain any foothold in the life of a person who has accepted Jesus and been born again of the Holy Spirit. Others would go to the opposite extreme, and ascribe all our troubles to demonic activity, spending a large part of their time hunting for demons and casting them out.[57]

The truth, as usual, lies between extremes. We need, again, to realize that we are three-part beings. Satan cannot invade the *spirit* of a Christian, because the Holy Spirit is living there. However, enemy forces, if allowed, can influence or invade the *soul*, the psychological part, to the degree that deliverance prayer is sometimes needed to expel them. A Christian can be depressed, oppressed, or obsessed by wrong spirits, but not *possessed*. In a possessed person, the entire being—spirit, soul, and body—is controlled by the enemy.

Close the Entrance

People still may ask, "Why do we have to concern ourselves with something like soul-healing prayer, when all we need do is cast out these evil spirits and all will be well?"

In recent years there seems to have been some cooling of enthusiasm for deliverance ministry, and I think I know one reason. It's discouraging to pray for someone for deliverance, see them helped, and then a few months later find them in even worse condition, because, presumably, the spirits who were cast out returned and found the house "swept and garnished," (Luke 11:25). What's the good of casting out spirits if they just come popping back, as they often seem to do? And *why* do they?

They come back because deliverance does not meet the whole need. Often the wrong spirits got in originally because of unhealed hurts in the soul—broken windows and smashed doors through which they found a way in. Not only do the spirits need to be cast out, but the soul needs to be healed to keep them from getting back in.

Some time ago we had mice. They were a nuisance. They got into food storage; they chewed on some of our furniture, and—most distressing—they died in out-of-the-way spots, creating awful smells! What did we do? We set traps for our furry invaders! We tried to get rid of them—chase them out, but they still kept coming back, until Dennis found the hole through which they were getting into the house. After he sealed that up, no more mice, and no more need to cast them out!

For instance, take a man with a violent temper. He has the temper because he's a hurt person. He gets angry because of what was done to him, perhaps very early in his life. His Hurt Child is angry. Through the emotions of that angry child, a spirit of anger may find access to the man's soul. Then, since he is not controlling his temper but letting it fly, the enemy is able to strengthen his position; he can bring the man more and more under his domination, perhaps getting him to do real violence to persons or property.

Or maybe the problem is sexual. Because of hurts in the inner child, there is a deep unfilled need for physical love, to be held and caressed. Through this door the enemy can introduce a spirit of insatiable sexual desire. In the grown person, this is expressed in a desperate need for physical affection. This may be shown by the man or woman being overdemanding of his or her mate in marriage, or in constant "girl-watching" in the man; or in a woman by her being "man crazy." Such people may seek to fantasize by watching X-rated movies and TV, or reading pornography of one sort or another. The more they indulge their fantasy, the stronger it grows, and the deeper hold the wrong spirits get on the soul.

Wherever a person seems to have little control over his thoughts or actions in a certain area or areas, or whenever he gives way to compulsive behavior, you may suspect the work of the enemy.

How to Pray About Compulsive Behavior

Some think you should pray for deliverance first, and then go on to soul healing. Others recommend the opposite. I believe, again, that you should be led by the Holy Spirit, as there are people who will not be able to recognize a need for deliverance until they have experienced some healing; while others will not be able to respond to healing until they have received some deliverance. Some won't need deliverance prayers at all, because after the soul healing, the wrong spirits will have lost their influence. With serious needs such as those just referred to, and other compulsive behavior patterns, the following procedure is recommended.

Whichever way you are led to go about it, your first preparation is your own self. *Make sure* you are walking in the light, that you have forgiven others, have been forgiven for anything wrong in your life, and that you are free from any wrong spiritual influence. Always have a prayer partner. This is a good plan in any case, but especially when praying for deliverance. If you're new to this kind of praying, get an experienced person to lead in praying, and you assist them. This is the safest way to learn.

To help a person who seems to need deliverance, here's a pattern to follow:

First, *lead him to ask forgiveness from God,* as described in the last chapter. Say, "Remember, even though you have sometimes not been able to control your compulsive wrong actions—losing your temper, getting sexually involved, and so forth—you were and are responsible for them. You need God's forgiveness. *And you must seek forgiveness from anyone you have hurt or offended,* and do your best to undo any harm you may have done by your wrong behavior. Even if you can't *feel* in your emotions that what you've done is wrong, take this step by faith."

After he has asked God to forgive him, *you should assure him of God's forgiveness,* using a Scripture such as 1 John 1:9: "*N.* [*using his name*], the Bible says, 'If you confess your sins, He is faithful and just, and will forgive you your sins, and cleanse you from all wrong.'[58] Since you have told God you are sorry for what you have done, He has forgiven you as He promised, and cleansed you through the blood of Jesus."

If the person you're to pray with is from a church that offers sacramental confession, encourage him to go to his priest or minister and receive absolution before he comes to pray with you.

Now, if you know what the particular need for deliverance is, you can lead the person to pray about it. I recommend that you show him how to pray for himself, while you pray in agreement with him. We find when we do it this way, there are not so likely to be startling manifestations or distressing physical reactions. There's no way to guarantee that such things will never happen—they did sometimes when Jesus prayed for people[59]—but you don't have to expect or encourage them. Most of all, *you don't have to regard them as necessary in order for the deliverance to be effective.*

Another reason for teaching people to do their own praying is that they will then know how to do it for themselves, when they don't have anyone to pray with them.

Have the person pray a simple prayer like this: "Spirit of [*anger, fear,* or *other*], I bind you under the blood of Jesus Christ. I command you to leave me, never to return, in Jesus' name."[60] You will usually find that the person, after casting out one spirit, will get the idea, and will recognize and name others that need to be dealt with. In any deliverance prayer, always be sure to speak the name of Jesus and invoke the power of His blood. There's no need to shout; just speak with authority.

After the spirits have been named and cast out, ask God's Holy Spirit to fill any empty places in the person's soul.

Now proceed with soul-healing prayer.

After soul-healing prayer, remind the person of the steps that were covered: "You confessed your sins; received forgiveness from God; promised to right any wrongs; cast out any evil spirits; and then we prayed for your soul to be healed." Say further:

"The next step is to use self-control to keep yourself from letting any hurts that are still unhealed control your actions. You're going to find it easier to do this because of the healing you've received today. If you still have problems, don't be discouraged, but go through these steps again, either with us or other prayer partners, or if that isn't possible, by yourself.

"You may find you have to repeat this series a number of times, especially if you have often given way to your inclinations, and formed habit patterns. As healing proceeds, you'll be more and more able to set your will in the right direction; the need for forgiveness and deliverance will become less and less; and your ability to control yourself will increase.

"Follow these steps whenever you find yourself being tempted, or if you should give way to temptation. Each one is important; you may not get to the top in one jump, but each step you take leads you higher toward the goal of complete healing and deliverance.

"You can use these steps, omitting the soul-healing prayer, if you aren't able to get it at the time of crisis. But do so as soon as possible."

A good deliverance Scripture is: "Lord God, other lords beside You have had dominion over us: but we will make men-tion of Your name. They are dead [wrong spirits cast out are as dead to us, being no more in control]; they shall not live [their works are stopped]; they are destroyed, and have made all their memory to perish [soul-healing prayer]."[61]

Every Christian Needs to Know

Every Christian, children included, should know his or her authority in Jesus, and how to pray at least for himself or his family. No person lives the way he or she should at all times; no one is without problems. Then, too, earth is still a battleground between good and evil, so we need to know how to resist the evil. Assault from the enemy is something every Christian will experience (Jesus Himself did), so we need to know what to do about it. The Bible says, "Therefore submit to God. Resist the devil and he will flee from you. Draw near to God and He will draw near to you . . ." (James 4:7, 8 NKJB-NT).

If you have received Jesus, and are living in the power of the Holy Spirit, you need have no fear of Satan and his helpers. In the name of the Lord, you have absolute authority over the forces of darkness. A lot of people have been terrified by the books and movies published in recent years exploiting exorcism. I hope it isn't necessary to point out that these are rather obviously inspired by the enemy himself to frighten people away from even trying to get delivered, or to help anyone else.

One of the points these books and movies emphasize is that deliverance prayer for others is dangerous. This could be true if the person praying is not a true believer. The Bible warning is in Acts 19:14, where the "seven sons of Sceva" get into hot water! They ordered the evil spirit to leave a possessed man in the name of Jesus, but they themselves had not accepted Jesus: "Then the man who had the evil spirit jumped on them and overpowered them all. He gave them such a beating . . ." (Acts 19:14 NIV). In other words, don't pray for someone for deliverance if you're not yourself a committed Christian, nor for a really possessed person without experienced help—except in a case of dire emergency. Jesus came to bring deliverance to the captives. All of us need to know how to pray this way, though some will be called to this work more than others.

I find, usually, when a person receives soul healing, the enemy leaves without my having to give him any attention. Specific prayer for deliverance is necessary when the person I'm praying with clearly needs to be set free before he or she can receive further healing, as would be the case with a compulsive person. It's a lot better looking at Jesus than casting out wrong spirits! On the other hand, I'm happy to pray deliverance prayers which make someone more open to God and His love.

Wrong Fantasy and the Hurt Person

A very hurt person may have a demonic fantasy world which began in childhood, and which he continues in from time to time as an adult. This comes because the person is so hurt he can't cope with life, and so tries to escape into fantasy. It may be connected with distorted sexual feelings. If you find this in a person, you will know he needs much soul healing, and probably deliverance. He may not at first be willing to let go of the fantasy, or even be able to see it as wrong, until he has received some healing. It can be helpful to talk with him about his fantasy world, since this may reveal much about what his hurts and needs are.

Sometimes it helps to treat the fantasy world in the same way we recommended in dealing with bad dreams and nightmares. See Jesus come into the scenes of the fantasy, and let

Him deal with them as He will. Sometimes the power of the wrong fantasy will crumble without any need for deliverance. Often, as Jesus is allowed into it, the powers of darkness leave without specific prayer against them. Where Jesus brings His light and truth, darkness has to leave.

Don't Repress It; Deal With It

Repress means to press something back so we don't have to look at it. When you keep saying to a hurt in your life, "I don't want to think about you, or even acknowledge you are there," you may succeed in forgetting it, and losing it in the basement of your library, but it's not really gone; it's still influencing you, but on a subconscious level. "Out of sight" isn't necessarily "out of mind."

At a retreat an attractive young woman in her early twenties came to a friend of ours for soul-healing help. She said, "Recently a lot of old painful memories have been surfacing, so I went to a minister to ask his advice. He just said, 'Forget it. Resist the enemy and he will flee.' "

The friend asked, "Are these real memories, or just a temptation of the enemy?"

The young woman replied, "They're real, all right. I had two abortions—the first was when I was sixteen. I've asked God to forgive me, but the shame, the fright, and the guilt, continue to come back to torment me. Every morning I wake up feeling guilty."

Our friend responded, "At certain times all that is needed is to resist the enemy's attack on your thought life with a simple prayer, but these are real memories, so God is letting you know you need further help in dealing with them."

They prayed, seeing Jesus in the doctor's office after her ordeal, helping this lost, scared teenager. In a very few minutes,

Jesus walked with her through the scene. Then she saw Jesus taking her little child home to heaven with Him. Jesus told her, "Your little boy is with Me and you will be reunited one day." Tears poured down her face, as she sobbed tears of release, and relief. When she gained her composure, she forgave the others involved in her troubles.

The day after prayer she reported, "I've seen several psychiatrists and received some help, but always the next day the burden of guilt was back. Today I woke up free from guilt for the first time in years. Time and again I'd asked God to forgive me, but now I *know* He has. I'm healed!"

We all have to temporarily *suppress* thoughts and emotions at times, so we can give our attention to something else. But continued *repression* of something that needs to be dealt with will never bring wholeness. To avoid repression we must be willing to face any valid thought or emotion. With Jesus this can be done safely and with full healing results.

Resisting Isn't Repressing

Resisting thoughts and temptations from the enemy is not the same as repressing. In this last example, the thought the woman needed to be healed from was a memory of something that had really happened. Evil thoughts that attack us from outside are a different matter. They're not real hurts that need healing. We can resist them and ignore them.

For about six years, in my early twenties, I was not walking closely with God. When I turned back to Him and was released in the Holy Spirit, I had a battle in my soul. For several weeks, weird and frightening thoughts would flash into my mind. I had gory nightmares! I went to a minister for help, thinking perhaps I needed deliverance.

"Rita," he said, "you don't need deliverance. What you need

is to memorize and apply this verse: 'Casting down [evil imaginations] and every high thing that exalts itself against the knowledge of God, bringing every thought into captivity to the obedience of Christ,' " (2 Corinthians 10:5 NKJB-NT).

I took his advice, and my thought battle got less and less, as my mind came more under the Lordship of Jesus. Now when wrong thoughts come along, I know what to do about them.

A good way to test any questionable thought is to ask yourself: *Is it from my recreated spirit? Is it from God? Is it from my soul, and should I pay attention to it as a problem needing to be healed? Or is it purely from the enemy, to be resisted and driven away?*

If you decide it's from Satan, resist it. Do what the preceding Scripture says: "I bind you, thought, in Jesus' name, and bring you into captivity. I am a new creature in Christ, and I won't permit you to take up lodging in me. Be gone in Jesus' name!" Then begin to praise God.

You need to know how to resist the enemy. Your children need to know, too, for their protection. In some ways your kids are more under attack than you, because they are still in their formative years, living in our rapidly deteriorating culture. Paul told the Ephesians (and you and me) to "put on the whole armor of God" (6:11). If there isn't a war on, why would God tell us to put on our battle gear?

Deliverance and soul healing work together; they are complementary. And after deliverance and soul-healing prayer, we need to remember there's an enemy to be resisted.

16

Free to Pass It On

POPCORN DISPENSERS

Christians are like popcorn dispensers—
They're filled with the good of the Lord,
But some are machines that are broken—
Others jam, and can't give of their hoard.

Some, like you, full of God's goodness,
Are functioning, willing to share,
May your life stay well oiled with the Spirit,
Servings rich, enjoyable—my prayer.[62]

RITA BENNETT

Father Ted Dobson says, "To seek help for myself may appear selfish to some, but without this help, I'm not free to reach out to others to help them." It is not self-centered to want to become whole. It's intelligent. It's obedient. It's letting Jesus do what He came to do. It's getting you strong enough to help others, and for the right reasons. It's wonderful to see people who have received healing eager to pass the blessing on.

Because soul healing isn't practicing psychology or psychiatry, but simply letting Jesus heal soul hurts, any person who wants to (and is beginning to be emotionally free himself) can pray for someone else. Even if you are yourself being prayed for, there's no reason you shouldn't be praying with others, provided you've come to a point in your own healing where you can give full attention to somebody else for an hour or so. In fact, if you have been, or are being prayed for yourself, it will help you in praying for others. You don't have to be "perfect" to help people—how well I know!

In this book, I'm not giving you fixed formulas but guidelines. I'm saying, "This is the way we *usually* do it." As with spelling, there will be exceptions to the rule. Remember to depend on the Holy Spirit and His gifts, especially wisdom, knowledge, and discernment. You may find that you develop favorite ways of praying, but follow the Spirit. Don't get so systematized that you forget to lean on His guidance.

Most of what I've told you has come from my own experience, while praying with people. As you meet different situations, God will give you creative direction. Only be sure what you say and do is in line with the Scripture.

Six Cautions to Keep You Balanced

1. Don't get too introspective, or encourage others to spend too much time looking inside. You need to look at your soul enough to get it healed, but you need to keep your eyes most of the time on your recreated spirit, where Jesus is living. Practice the presence of Jesus, not the presence of your soul.

Self-examination is important, though. Examining yourself is safe when you're being led by the gentle Holy Spirit. Psalms 139:23, 24 says: "Search me, O God, and know my heart: try me, and know my thoughts: And see if there be any wicked way in me, and lead me in the way everlasting."

The philosopher Plato said, "The unexamined life is not worth living." I wouldn't feel that strongly about it, but it is important. It's unfortunate when your life is so busy and active, that you don't have time to evaluate it.

Each day examine your inner self briefly, and from time to time take a deeper look as the Holy Spirit leads (during soul-healing prayer with friends, for example), or before coming to the Lord's Table. Paul teaches us to examine our lives before receiving Holy Communion (1 Corinthians 11:28, 29). Again, Jesus said, "Leave your gift at the altar; go and be reconciled with your brother; then come and offer your gift" (Matthew 5:24, *paraphrased*). Paul also said that if we judged ourselves we would not be judged or corrected by the Lord (*see* 1 Corinthians 11:31, 32).

Balance your introspection by thinking and rejoicing about God's love for you, and the hurts God has healed and is healing.

2. Don't try to dig into your own or someone else's subconscious memories. Let the Holy Spirit bring things up. Don't rush. He knows the right time and place. Don't look for techniques to force the subconscious to release material. Remember again, you're just God's office boy or girl, helping Him do what He wants to do. Pray only for those hurts that have clearly surfaced.

Remember Dave, whom we discussed earlier. He had remarkable healing because God the Holy Spirit brought up and helped him deal with events which he could not possibly have remembered. The people praying with him did not dig these memories up, nor could they have known anything about them.

Don't pray for the most hurtful memory first. If several memories surface, take the one easiest to handle first.

3. When praying for yourself or others, be careful of any judgmental attitudes creeping in. Our judgments are at best limited. When tempted to judge another remind yourself: "If I had been born into the same family, at the same time, of the same sex, with the same environment and hurts, I likely would have had the same or even worse problems."

If someone on the team has a broken leg, you don't say, "Here, catch the ball, run down the field, and make a touchdown!" You know you'd be asking the impossible. Treat people with emotional handicaps with as much consideration. Don't say, "You can do it if you just *try* hard enough."

In a sermon at Saint Alban's Episcopal Church, Edmonds, Washington, Father George Wilson was speaking to this subject. In essence he said, "Jesus said, 'Wheat and tares will grow together to the end.' There's a particular weed called 'darnel,' which looks much like wheat, and it's hard to tell the difference. God tells us in the garden of His world we're not to weed but to love. If we love a lot, the wheat may grow so well it may take over many of the weeds!"

Easy on the weeding and pour on the love instead!

4. Don't manipulate. Don't try to direct what the person should visualize. The Holy Spirit will direct. God doesn't change the past. Remember, though, we record in our memories not just what happened, but how we *felt* about it and interpreted it. It is this Jesus alters and heals.

In Reliving the Scene With Jesus Prayer, we aren't trying to escape memories, but are seeing how God can and will redeem them. It's like two photographs. The old memory becomes a faded picture, while the new one Jesus gives is in vivid color. He always overcomes the plans of the evil one with good, when allowed to. And sometimes, as in Creative Prayer, He establishes a brand-new memory which is outside the old.

5. Keep confidences. Never tell anyone what was told you in a prayer session, unless you have clear permission to do so. This is why it's good to have a prayer partner to talk and pray with. If you share private information, without permission, you can cause more damage than if you hadn't prayed at all. Yes, God can heal that, too, but here prevention is far better than cure!

6. Be in a church fellowship under the leadership of a faithful and loving pastor. Let him know what you're doing, and ask him to take part if he's interested. It will be great if a group of people become involved in a soul-healing ministry at your church.

Ten Steps to Healing

By way of review let's see what these ten steps are:

1. Recognize your need.[63]

2. Desire help.[64]

3. Read Scripture and books on soul healing. (*See* list at the back of this book.)

4. Share your hurts.[65]

5. Know that God is unconditional love.[66]

6. Realize God is omnipresent.[67]

7. By faith see or sense Jesus in the scene.[68]

8. Hear what Jesus speaks to you and others.[69]

9. If someone is praying with you, tell what you see and hear.[70]

10. Forgive and speak forgiveness.[71] (Ask forgiveness where you, too, realize you were wrong.)[72]

The Past and Present

Soul healing is not for the purpose of encouraging you to live in the past; it's to bring you into the joy of living *now*. It's your hurts that make you live in the past; when they are dealt with, you'll move into the "now."

"Forgetting the past . . . I press on," says Paul to the Philippians (*see* 3:13, 14). Trying to forget or repress past hurts makes it all the more sure that you won't, but as old memories and emotions are healed, you can let them go.

The ultimate goal of soul healing is that we should realize and visualize Jesus with us in the present moment, so that as soon as we are hurt, we may get healed then and there—and forgive right away, too. Jesus did not delay to forgive. He was the Master of unconditional forgiveness. As He was being crucified, He cried out, "Father, forgive them; for they know not what they do . . ." (Luke 23:34). Stephen, filled with the Holy Spirit, and seeing Jesus at the right hand of the Father as he was being killed said, "Lord, don't blame them for this!" (*see* Acts 7:59, 60). Jesus said, "You'll have troubles in this world," but He adds, "Cheer up! I have overcome the world!" (John 16:33, *paraphrased*).

Nicolas Heman of Lorraine, commonly known as "Brother Lawrence," was a humble lay brother in a Carmelite Monastery in Paris in the 1600s. The widely known book *The Practice of the Presence of God* describes how he sought always to be aware of Jesus, no matter where he was or what he was doing. He said "In the noise and clatter of my kitchen, while several persons are at the same time calling for different things, I possess God in as great tranquillity, as if I were upon my knees at the blessed sacrament."[73]

At this very moment, by faith acknowledge Jesus' presence with you and think about Him. It may be hard at first, because of distractions, to concentrate very long, but don't let that discourage you. Instead of having moments thinking of nothing in particular, think about Jesus. Remember God is with you when you doubt yourself, as well as when you feel great. When you experience rejections, remember He is there. Listen deep within to God as He speaks assurances of love to you. "You are My child. I love you. I believe in you."

Brother Lawrence lived in a monastery. We can practice this same relationship with the Lord while being out in the world, caring for and helping others to know Him too. Our hurts have often sidetracked us from the work to which God has called us. As we are healed in our souls, we can get our eyes off ourselves, and effectively be "about our Father's business."

The Future

Do you know you can practice Jesus' presence in your future, too? I learned this while praying with a man who was very depressed and fearful about an upcoming business meeting.

"Jack,"[74] I said, "Jesus is in the future as well as the past and present. Let's ask Him to reassure you by showing you He's going to be with you in that meeting you're so worried about."

As we prayed, he saw the room and the businessmen gathered there, and Jesus standing close by. When the actual meeting took place several days later, Jack was relaxed, and said it was one of the best and easiest sessions he'd had for some time. No, we weren't trying to peek into the future, but were simply asking to know and sense Jesus' presence in that coming event.

Especially these days, people are fearful of the future, but Jesus can give hope for the future too. One woman, as she was healed, said, "Now that I see Jesus working in my life and loving me all the way from the beginning to this present moment, I can have hope for the days ahead."

Jesus wants us to live in the present with hope for the future.

Set Free

Soul-healing prayer is not the answer to everything. It doesn't replace the other truths which a Christian ought to "know and believe to his soul's health," as the old prayer book put it:[75] worshiping and praising God; receiving the Lord's Supper; reading the Scriptures; enjoying fellowship with other believers, intercessory prayer; helping people in need; and so forth. It doesn't replace these, and remember, *every* experience with Jesus brings inner healing. No, soul-healing prayer isn't the only way to be healed, but it is a most effective one.

My original definition of soul healing was "Practicing the presence of Jesus in your past as well as in the present, and on into the future—helping you forgive everyone, and *setting you free* to live in the present at your fullest potential."

One of the great words in the Bible is *freedom.* God wants you free to be yourself, not what someone else wanted or wants you to be—not bound in your emotions and memories but free and unimpeded.

He wants you to find out who you are, and to enjoy being you. He wants you to be free to love Him with all your being, just as He loves you. Free to love yourself, your family, and your neighbors. Free to cry, to love, to laugh. Free to give of yourself to others. Free to know "all things work together for good." Free to reach your highest goals. He wants you free from the negatives of the past, free to look ahead with joy, free to live in the now.

He wants you to be . . .
                    Emotionally Free!

Source Notes

Chapter 1   The Beginning
1. Name has been changed. 2. Name has been changed.

Chapter 2   Jim Moves Ahead
2a. Name has been changed.
2b. Name has been changed.
3. Dale R. Jordan, *Dyslexia in the Classroom* (Columbus: Ohio: Charles E. Merrill Publishing Company, 1972), p. 3.

Chapter 3   Psyche and Spirit
4. *See* Genesis 1:26, 27; 5:3; 9:6.
5. Quoted by Dr. Thomas A. Harris in *I'm OK—You're OK* (London: Jonathan Cape, 1973); Pan paperback, 1973, p. 27.

Chapter 4   Do You Need Soul Healing?
6. By a *qualified* professional, I mean one with the best skill and education possible; a committed Christian, led by the Holy Spirit. If a Christian isn't available, a non-Christian may be acceptable, provided he or she will not try to tamper with the faith of the counselee.
7. R. C. Trench, *Synonyms of the New Testament* (Grand Rapids, Michigan: Wm. B. Eerdmans Sons, 1953), p. 246. Scholars please note that the King James translators would have been using the older Greek manuscript, probably the so-called *Textus Receptus* (actually there were probably several manuscripts known by this name). The later versions do not have *paraptoma* here, but the more common *hamartia*.
8. John 1:33; Acts 1:5; 2:1–4; 8:5–17; 10:44–48; 11:15–17; 19:1–7. For further discussion on this subject, read *The Holy Spirit and You* Dennis and Rita Bennett (Kingsway Publications, 1971).

Chapter 6   Teach Us to Pray
9. *Macbeth*, Act III, Scene 2.
10. *See* Matthew 26:73, 74; Mark 14:70–72; Luke 22:55–62.
11. Ruth Stapleton was probably the first person to point out in her book *The Gift of Inner Healing* that Peter's denial and then his positive confession both took place in front of a charcoal fire. She also notes that a

"charcoal fire" is only mentioned in these two places in the New Testament. The look of the fire; its warmth on that cold night, and the smell of it, too, would all have been deeply imprinted in Peter's memory; and the look and feel and smell of the fire on the beach on that cold morning would certainly have brought it all back.

12. (Plainfield, N.J.: Logos International, 1973), pp. 120, 121.

13. The Rev. John Sandford of Coeur d'Alene, Idaho, is well known for his counseling ministry, and for his writings. He is the coauthor, with his wife, Paula, of *Restoring the Christian Family*, Logos International, 1979, and other books.

Chapter 7   Your Hurt Child of the Past

14. Cecil Osborne, *Release From Fear and Anxiety* (Waco, Texas: Word Books, 1976), p. 137.

15. The helpful teaching on the parent, adult, and child developed through the late Dr. Eric Berne would be a good example. It has been most helpful.

16. Osborne, *op. cit.*, p. 182

17. Name has been changed.

18. Name has been changed.

19. "The Hebrew *na'ar* could be used of an infant, as of Moses in the ark of bulrushes (Exodus 2:6); at the other extreme, it was used of a young man of marriageable age, as of Absalom during his revolt against David (2 Samuel 18:5; cf. Genesis 34:19). We cannot, therefore, derive from this verse the exact age of Jeremiah at the time of his call. The LXX renders 'I am too young.' " *The Interpreter's Bible*, volume 5 (Nashville, Tennessee: Abingdon Press, 1977), p. 801.

Chapter 8   Your Creative Inner Child

20. Osborne, *op. cit.*, p. 63.

21. *The Book of Common Praise*, Anglican Church of Canada, revised 1938, pp. 742, 743.

22. Jose Luis Carreno, S. D. B., *Shroud of Christ*, © 1980, pp. 8, 9.

23. Denis Thomas, *The Face of Christ* (Garden City, New York: Doubleday & Co., Inc., 1979), p.51.

24. Ruth Carter Stapleton shared this insight on tapes which accompanied the Leader's Guide to her book *The Experience of Inner Healing*.

25. Name has been changed.

26. John Powell, S. J., *The Secret of Staying in Love* (Niles, Illinois: Argus Communications, 1974).

Chapter 9 Parents Are Important

27. This poem was written by Dr. William S. Reed in 1938, when he was fifteen years old. My brother, Bill, wrote this after the rest of our family had moved to Florida, leaving him in Michigan to finish school and enter the university.

28. Some women readers may be thinking, *That leaves me out. I've never had children.* To you I would say there are so many young people desperately in need of parent figures to help them grow psychologically, that even if you, as I, haven't had children of your own, you can "mother" someone else's! If your own children are raised and gone, you can continue to use your wealth of experience to help other young people.

29. Dale Douglas Mills, cover story, "Are the Seeds of Suicide Planted During Babyhood?" *The Seattle* [Washington] *Times Magazine*, September 23, 1979.

30. The New International Version, the New English Bible, the New American Standard Bible, and the Good News Bible translate "kept" as "treasured." The New Amplified Bible reads, ". . . . his mother kept and closely and persistently guarded all these things in her heart."

31. Dennis and Rita Bennett, *Trinity of Man* (Plainfield, N.J.: Logos International, 1979).

32. William L. Vaswig, *I Prayed, He Answered* (Minneapolis, Minnesota: Augsburg Publishing House, 1977), p. 19.

33. Paul says, ". . . If God be for us, who can be against us?" (Romans 8:31).

34. Robert Frost, *Set My Spirit Free*, pp. 9, 10.

35. *Ibid.*, p. 4.

36. A. A. Milne, *The House at Pooh Corner* (London: Methuen 1928), p. 278.

Chapter 10 Adults Hurt, Too

37. Dennis Bennett, *Nine O'clock in the Morning* (Kingsway Publications, 1971), pp. 144–154.

38. Vaswig, *op. cit.*, p. 104.

39. Name has been changed.

40. Some may say at this point, "How could Jesus tell the young man this, since he had committed suicide and therefore must have been in hell?" The idea that suicide is an unforgivable sin does not come from the New Testament, but from later interpretations, especially Saint Augustine. There is nothing in the Bible that says suicide is necessarily unforgivable. I'm not saying this, of course, to justify suicide, but to point out that it is not the act itself, but the condition of the person committing the act that

must concern us. This we are totally unable to judge, nor do we have the right to do so.

Chapter 11   Getting to the Roots

41. Names have been changed.

42. J. A. Stringham, *The Mind, the Original Computer* (Chicopee, Massachusetts: The School of Pastoral Care, 1978), p. 103.

43. *Fetus* is from the Latin word meaning "fruitful" or "newly delivered."

44. This information was taken from the sleeve of the record "Lullaby From the Womb," created by Dr. Hajime Murooka and produced by Capitol Records, Inc., 1975. Dr. Murooka developed this record to assist newborns adjusting from the sound within the mother to their new environment, helping them get a better start. Because the babies are calmed by the record, mothers are helped too.

45. Frederic Leboyer, *Birth Without Violence* (London: Wildwood House, 1975), p. 15.

46. *Ibid.*, p. 103.

47. Name has been changed.

49. Research has demonstrated pulsation of the unborn's heart at the twenty-first day.

50. Psalms 139:13 *paraphrased. Reins* according to *Webster's New Collegiate Dictionary* 1980 means: ". . . the region of the kidneys . . . the seat of the feelings or passions." Formerly the kidneys were thought of as the source of the temperament. "Think of that, a man of my kidney . . ." (Sir John Falstaff, *The Merry Wives of Windsor*, Act III, Sc. 5). The Latin derivation of "reins" is from *renes*, kidneys. It seems possible there is a relationship between the word *reins* and "rein," as in the reins of a horse. This kind of "rein" probably comes from the Latin *retinere*, to restrain, through the Middle French word *rene* which certainly is close to *renes*. In any case, it would seem quite logical to associate the "reins" with the subconscious mind, the hidden controller of the temperament.

Chapter 12   A New Start for Susie

51. I didn't find out until after our prayer times were over that Susie's next sister, Vicki, born only thirteen months after her, had spent the first five months of her life in the hospital, so Susie necessarily spent a lot of time with a baby-sitter. Her mother s aid, "When we picked Susie up after we had been at the hospital with Vicki, we were so anxious, we could hardly be described as ideal parents." Being separated from her parents again so soon, when scarcely a year old, would surely have added to previ-

ous feelings of estràngement and perhaps unimportance. It occurred to me, too, that Susie's refusal to eat might be a regression to earliest infancy, going back to where she felt secure. If so, it wasn't hard to see why she was trying to live on milk alone.

Chapter 13   How to Pray for Your Children and Your Family
52. Leboyer, *Birth Without Violence*, p. 21.

53. The book *A Child Is Born* by Dr. Ahel Ingelman-Sundberg, an obstetrician (Delacorte Press, 1977), would be an excellent help, as well as Leboyer's book. Both have fine pictures children would understand.

54. Quote from F. W. Boreham, *A Bunch of Everlastings* (London: Judson Press, 1949), pp. 201, 202.

Chapter 14   How to Forgive
55. Name has been changed.

Chapter 15   Deliverance Brings Healing
56. C. S. Lewis, *The Screwtape Letters* (London: Macmillan & Co. Inc., 1971, reprint; Fontana paperback 1970), p. 9.

57. A good Scripture for balance here is: ". . . . I want you to be wise as to what is good, and simple concerning evil" (Romans 16:19 NKJB-NT).

58. This is a paraphrase of 1 John 1:9.

59. Mark 9:20, 26, and other Scripture references.

60. In the Scriptures, demonic spirits are usually named by their predominant activity or vice. Mark 9:25 is one example.

61. This is a paraphrase of Isaiah 26:13, 14,

Chapter 16   Free to Pass It On
62. Inspired by the verse "Out of Order" by André Auw, quoted by John Powell in *The Secret of Staying in Love*, pp. 11, 12.

63. Mark 9:24.

64. Mark 10:46–52.

65. James 5:16. In soul healing, we like to have two people praying with each person, if possible, as this gives more opportunity for the Hqly Spirit to minister His gifts. Jesus set the pattern of working "two by two" (Luke 10:1), and we've experienced the wisdom of His doing so.

66. *See* John 10:10; 15:9; 17:26; 1 John 3:1; 3:16; 4:7, 8; Jeremiah 31:3; Luke 11:11–13; 15:11–24; 1 Corinthians 13:4–8.

67. *See* Psalms 139:5–10, 13; Jeremiah 23:23, 24; Proverbs 15:3; Acts 17:27, 28; Hebrews 13:8; Romans 8:35–39.

68. *See* Proverbs 3:6; 2 Corinthians 5:16; Luke 24:13–45; Hebrews 11:1.

69. *See* John 10:27; 18:37.

70. *See* Romans 10:10; Mark 5:19.

71. *See* Mark 11:25.

72. *See* Matthew 5:23, 24.

73. *The Practice of the Presence of God*, Fourth Conversation.

74. Name has been changed.

75. *Book of Common Prayer*, 1928 (crown copyright), p. 277.

Bibliography

Ingleman-Sundberg, Ahel (photography by Lennart Nilsson), *A Child Is Born*, New York: Dell Publishing Co., Inc., 1966.

Leboyer, Frederick, *Birth Without Violence*, London: Wildwood House, 1975; Fontana paperback, 1977.

Osborne, Cecil, *Release From Fear and Anxiety*, Waco, Texas: Word Books, 1976.

Powell, John, S. J., *Unconditional Love*, Niles, Illinois: Argus Communications, 1978.

Other Suggested Reading

Bennett, Dennis and Rita, *The Holy Spirit and You*, Kingsway Publications, 1971.

——, *Trinity of Man*, Plainfield, N.J.: Logos International, 1979.

Dobson, Theodore Elliott, *Inner Healing: God's Great Assurance*, New York: Paulist Press, 1978.

MacNutt, Francis, *Healing Through Prayer*, abridged from *Healing*, New York: Bantam Books, 1977.

Nee, Watchman, *Release of the Spirit*, Ministry of Life, Box 74—Route 2, Cloverdale, Indiana 46120: Sure Foundation, 1965.

Payne, Leanne, *The Broken Image*, Westchester, Illinois: Cornerstone Books, 1981.

Powell, John, S. J., *The Secret of Staying in Love*, Niles, Illinois: Argus Communications, 1974.

Reed, William S., M.D., *Healing of the Whole Man—Mind, Body, Spirit* (formerly titled *Surgery of the Soul, 1969*), Old Tappan N.J., Spire Books, Fleming H. Revell Company, 1979.

Stapleton, Ruth Carter, *The Experience of Inner Healing*, Sevenoaks: Hodder & Stoughton, 1978.

Vaswig, William L., *I Prayed, He Answered*, Minneapolis, Minnesota: Augsburg Publishing House, 1977.

Index

Also in paperback from Kingsway . . . ▬

How to Pray for Inner Healing
for yourself and others

by Rita Bennett

Emotional wounds are not easy to heal. In this book Rita Bennett provides basic training for helping people who are emotionally distressed.

Building on the foundations laid in her earlier book *Emotionally Free*, Rita gives practical guidelines on how to minister sensitively to the needs of others. In so doing, we may discover for ourselves too the healing that the Lord Jesus offers to those who turn to Him.

Rita Bennett is co-author with her husband Dennis of THE HOLY SPIRIT AND YOU.

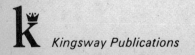

Kingsway Publications

Available from your usual Christian book supplier, or Mail Order enquiries to: Charisma Christian Mail Order, P.O. Box 77, Hailsham, E. Sussex BN27 3EF.

Moving on in the Spirit

by Dennis Bennett

All over the world Christians have been experiencing a new love for God and a new freedom in praise and worship. Gifts of healing have been rediscovered, and churches have come alive by the renewing work of the Spirit.

This book starts from there. It encourages us to continue on the course that God has set, but also points out some of the pitfalls which lie in our path.

Dennis Bennett challenges some of the wrong ideas that are infiltrating many Christian circles today—including misunderstandings about praise, healing, and the acceptance of all things as God's will.

Knowing the truth on such important issues will enable us to 'think the thoughts of God', helping us to understand his purposes and so move on in the Spirit.

Dennis Bennett is the author of the bestseller
Nine O'Clock in the Morning,
and (with his wife Rita),
The Holy Spirit and You.

Kingsway Publications